MW00678997

The Polishing Cloth

Eighteenth Edition

Georgia Perimeter College

Editors

Kenneth McNamara

Nancy Kojima ◆ Na Keya H. Bazemore

Kendall Hunt

publishing company

Cover image © Shutterstock, Inc.

www.kendallhunt.com
Send all inquiries to:
4050 Westmark Drive
Dubuque, IA 52004-1840

Copyright © 1992, 1993, 1994, 1995, 1996, 1997, 1998, 1999, 2000, 2001, 2002, 2004, 2005, 2007, 2009, 2011, 2012, 2013 by Georgia Perimeter College

ISBN 978-1-4652-1149-1

Kendall Hunt Publishing Company has the exclusive rights to reproduce this work, to prepare derivative works from this work, to publicly distribute this work, to publicly perform this work and to publicly display this work.

All rights reserved. No part of this publication may be reproduced, stored in a retrieval system, or transmitted, in any form or by any means, electronic, mechanical, photocopying, recording, or otherwise, without the prior written permission of the copyright owner.

Printed in the United States of America
10 9 8 7 6 5 4 3 2 1

Contents

♦♦♦

Freshman Composition

Sophomore Composition

The Polishing Cloth

Editorial Board

♦♦♦

Reggie Abbott

Na Keya Bazemore

Kathleen DeMarco

Michael Diebert

Richard Diguette

Valerie Dotson

Sherry Durren

Hank Eidson

James Faucett

Alicia Guarracino

Barbara Hall

Michael Hall

Jean Hakes

Ken Johnson

Nancy Kojima

Muriel Lange

Sarah Larson

Kenneth McNamara

Scott Mitchell

Stuart Noel

Carole Raybourn

Tamara Shue

Lita Hooper-Simanga

Kim Sisson

Corbin Stephens

Kirk Swenson

Ted Wadley

Shellie Sims-Welch

Preface

◆◆◆

"The responsibility of a writer is to excavate the experience of the people who produced him." – James Baldwin

The Eighteenth edition of *The Polishing Cloth* is a representation of what Georgia Perimeter College students and the editorial board embodies as extremely high quality essays. Students face so many challenges in writing, and this text proves that they can overcome these challenges. As the editor of this edition, I am very proud of each and every student who has been published. I congratulate you, and you should congratulate yourself as a published author.

The Polishing Cloth, a collection of the best essays at Georgia Perimeter College, was founded by Sarah Larsen in 1984. It covers a range of studies. As editors, we begin the text with our developmental studies classes and end with our sophomore classes.

I would like to thank the entire editorial board of the Eighteenth edition of *The Polishing Cloth*. The students and I could not have done this without your extreme dedication. Deciding what essays will be published is a difficult task. However, it brings me so much pleasure to notify a student that he or she has been selected for publication. I sometimes get screams of joy, I sometimes get tears of joy, yet my response is always the same, "You did this!"

I hope you all will enjoy the selections in the Eighteenth edition. We had several submissions that were of superb quality. I know that it is often hard to share work publically, but the students in this edition are unique, honest, and extremely brilliant. These are Georgia Perimeter College students.

On a personal note, I have so much to be thankful for. I was given the opportunity to be the editor of this edition. It is not the easiest task, but it is one that I am extremely honored to have had.

Colleagues are like family to me. Without you, I would not have had the power and strength to assist in producing this product. I would like to personally thank my Department Chair, Michael Hall. He guided me through this process with ease. Michael calmed me down when my head was spinning and showed me that there was light at the end of the tunnel. Na Keya Bazemore…you are my colleague, my go to person, but most of all, you are my dearest friend. I thank you both for all of your assistance, support, and dedication.

The Polishing Cloth's editorial board has grown immensely with this edition. I know that it is not always easy to read essays that are not from your own students. Time is always a factor. The time that you have given to me is a gift that I will never forget.

As we move into the Nineteenth edition of *The Polishing Cloth*, I wish the new editor, Nancy Kojima, much success. I also encourage all of Georgia Perimeter College students to look inside your souls. This is when you produce quality essays. I want each and every one of you to remember that writing can be therapeutic. Good luck to all of you submitting to the next edition. I look forward to reading your essays as I continue to serve on the editorial board.

Kenneth McNamara, Editor

My Best Qualities

Ashleigh Jones
ENGL 0099
♦♦♦

While growing up, I had a lot of friends. For some reason, people have always been attracted to me. In school, I was very shy and did not talk much, and most times a person would have to approach me to start a conversation. Once the conversation started, and we found out we had things in common, we would instantly become friends. Now that I am an adult, I realize that I have certain qualities that make me stand out from the rest. Being able to accept people for who they are, being understanding, and being confident in my own skin are some of my best qualities.

One of my best qualities is being able to accept people for who they are. For instance, back in middle school, there was a girl in my class whom no one got along with. When we had group assignments, no one wanted her to be in the group. When it was lunch time, no one sat with her, and students often teased her and called her names. One day, a friend and I took the liberty of talking to her just to find out why no one liked her. I found out that she had poor living conditions and low self-esteem. From that day on, all three of us became friends. I do not discriminate against people, and I do not judge. This is why I have friends from all different types of backgrounds.

Another quality I would consider to be my best is the fact that I am very understanding. There is nothing anyone can say to me that would shock me. I guess this is why people find me easy to talk to. For example, I am the friend whom everyone confides in. My friends tell me everything, including the stuff that makes them look bad. I am also caring and sensitive to other peoples' needs. I will go above and beyond for a friend or family member who needs me, sometimes even neglecting my own needs. At times, I can be very caring. People often tell me I know exactly what to say to make them feel better or think things through more, even when it is the hard truth.

The quality that stands out to be one of my best is that I am comfortable in my own skin. I feel that this is my best quality yet. I am not superficial, and I do not try to put up any "fronts" for anyone. I have high self-esteem, and I am confident about who I am. When people get to know me, they quickly realize that what you see is what you get. I love just being myself, and I think people who are around me can sense that as well. My friends always tell me that over the years while some friends have been "fake" and become distant, I was the one who stayed true.

Over the years, I have come to learn a lot about myself. I have gained knowledge through experience and through other people. Some of these experiences have allowed me to possess the qualities I have today. Even though I have several good qualities, accepting others for who they are, being understanding, and being comfortable in my own skin are some of the best qualities about me.

***

Why I Like This Essay: In this essay, Ashleigh does a great job of applying the formula for a successful traditional essay. She has a clear thesis and essay map, strong topic sentences, and good real world examples. She also does a great job of establishing her own voice here and convincing the reader that she does actually have the qualities she discusses; therefore, she gives the reader great examples to follow both in composition and life skills.
Dr. Valerie Dotson, Professor of English

Moving to America

Jeong Kim
ENGL 0099

♦♦♦

Although my family moved from South Korea to the United States more than ten years ago, I still remember the day we decided to move like it was yesterday. My move to the United States of America was the most memorable event that I have ever experienced.

After my father announced that we were going to move, our family got together and started to pack. It felt very strange packing up all the belongings in the house that I grew up in. My father left for America long before my mother, sister, and I. Due to this, my mother, being the most organized person in the family, packed most of our things. My sister and I helped my mother by being quiet and staying out of her way. We had far too many belongings, so we could not bring all of our things to America. So in order to take what was needed, we had a yard sale in front of our house to sell objects such as big furniture and appliances that were all in neat condition. After holding the yard sale and sending our luggage to our new home in America, we were all set and ready to take off to the land of dreams.

When I got to the In-Chon International Airport in Korea, the surroundings had hit me and made me realize that we were permanently moving to a different country. I started to panic. I panicked because I knew that I would not be able to see my friends and relatives for quite some time. However, my mother calmed me down by telling me I would be able to see everyone soon, but it would not be as much as before. She also told me about the things I would experience once I landed in and lived in America. For example, I would make new friends, try out new kinds of foods, and most importantly, experience a new fascinating culture. After a very long chat with my mother, I was happy and ready to depart. I felt very thrilled, and I was especially excited for the plane ride. After saying farewell to my friends and relatives, I boarded the plane and was finally on my way to America.

When I arrived at the Chicago O'Hare Airport, everything looked incredibly unusual. People around me were speaking in a funny language that I could not understand. Also, most of the signs were written in English, a language that I had never learned. Later, my mother told me it was a language I would learn to speak, read, and write in order to make friends and live in this country comfortably. It was a little hard for me to comprehend everything at once, but I was excited about meeting new people by learning a new language.

Looking out of a car window as we were driving to our new home, I noticed how the environment outside looked very different from where I used to live. Everywhere I looked, I saw farms and lots of trees which were very rare to find in the urban side of Seoul, South Korea. We finally arrived to our neighborhood where our new home was located. It looked foreign to me, but I was still thrilled to start a new life.

Although it has been over ten years since our family moved from South Korea to the United States, I still remember the day we decided to move like it was yesterday. Even though at first it was hard to transition from my life in Korea to another country, I have learned to love both South Korea and the United States equally. I am very glad our family decided to move to America because I experienced a once in a lifetime opportunity.

***

Why I Like This Essay: As an English learning support student, Jeong (Paul) exemplified mastery composition skills. In particular, his essay, "Moving to America," not only appealed to my visual imagery, but it was appealing to me how well he organized the essay. I liked how Paul's essay read like a true narrative. It has a clear beginning, middle, and end. I liked how he briefly and vividly narrated his experience of moving from Korea to America. Through his essay, readers are able to get a glimpse of how transitioning from one country to another may not always be easy, but how one must adapt to his or her new surroundings. Overall, Paul's essay pointed to his own

determination at learning a new language, which in turn shows through his work ethic and writing.
Danielle C. Heliton, Instructor of English

My Hobby

Joshua Emeter
ENGL 0099

◆◆◆

A hobby is a particular activity, which a person likes engaging in. Everyone has his or her own favorite hobby. For instance, my older sister's favorite hobby is reading. My sister could spend a whole day reading a novel or a magazine. Also, my younger brother's favorite hobby is playing video games. My brother spends at least 8 hours every day playing video games. I and my family members nicknamed him, "The Gamer." I have many hobbies, such as, swimming, singing, dancing, and so on, but my favorite hobby is playing soccer because it is fun, social, and it keeps me fit.

I love playing soccer because it is fun. Soccer is the most watched sport in the world. This is probably because it is very entertaining. Anytime I play soccer, I always want to score a goal. For example, I tried out for the soccer team at my previous school. Just after 10 minutes of trying out, I was chosen to join the school soccer team. The coach told me that he chose me solely because I have the zeal to score goals. This attitude of always trying to score may have come across as selfish playing to my team mates, but unfortunately, it is difficult for me to suppress that attitude because scoring goals is one of the reasons playing soccer is fun to me. Also, when I am playing soccer, it is very exciting to exhibit dribbling skills against my opponent. It is thrilling for both viewers and me. Performing skills during a soccer match is very fun.

Playing soccer is also my favorite hobby because there is social interaction. Soccer brings people together. For example, two of my friends had a huge argument, so they refused to talk to each other. As a result, I invited both of them to play soccer with me. At first, they refused to be on the same team, so I had to persuade them, and they eventually agreed to be on the same team. As the soccer match commenced, they soon began to communicate and work with one another during the match.

When our team scored, I saw my friends hugging and smiling at each other. Playing soccer ended the feud between my friends and re-united them again. Another example of how playing soccer promotes social interaction is seen when team mates of different races, ethnic groups, or backgrounds come together and socialize. There is no such thing as racism or a superior ethnic group in soccer. In soccer, people are judged by their skill in the game and not by their backgrounds. Playing soccer is a good socializing agent because it brings individuals of different backgrounds together.

The main reason playing soccer is my favorite hobby is because it keeps me fit. Soccer is a very competitive game, and it cannot be played by just anyone. Playing soccer requires physical fitness. Constant training is required to be physically fit. For instance, when I was on a soccer team, every Saturday, my team mates and I were to come to school for soccer training. This weekly training was to keep us physically fit. Also, when I am playing soccer, I am always on the run because anything can happen at any moment. This continuous running keeps my body fit.

Soccer has all the qualities I look for in a hobby. Soccer can be played by everyone. Soccer is a family friendly sport, and it can be played by all races and ethnic groups. Excitement, social interaction, and keeping fit are reasons why soccer is my favorite hobby.

***

Why I Like This Essay: This is an excellent ENGL 0099 essay because it is well-written in every regard. It begins with an interesting lead-in technique that modifies the "start with an opposite" approach by listing the hobbies of his family members, which begins to build the readers' curiosity about what his hobby might be. Then he clearly identifies his own hobby and why he loves it with a clear thesis and essay map. He then does an excellent job of supporting his topic sentences with relevant, interesting examples that help us to truly relate to his love for soccer. Who wouldn't want a hobby that could facilitate all of the things he has been able to accomplish through soccer?
Dr. Valerie Dotson, Professor of English

Qualities of a Good Student

Tiara Marie VanLowe
ENGL 0099
♦♦♦

Everyone knows that one student, who always talks about partying, never studies, barely attends class, and somehow wonders how he or she is not passing his or her class. A student with such bad student traits should learn and practice the qualities of a good student. A good student always comes to class on time, is attentive, and studies.

A good student always comes to class on time. It is important to be on time for class because once class has started, a student walking into class late becomes a distraction to the rest of the class. When a student arrives late for his or her class, the student misses parts of the lesson. It is never possible to learn without a lesson, so it is imperative to arrive on or before class starts. It is also good to be on time so that a student can ask questions if need be. For example, I went to my class late and could not ask a question because time did not permit in the class; there is no guarantee that I will be able to email my teacher and get the response or understanding to my questions. A good student plans his or her time before his or her class starts, so there is no delay in getting to class on time.

Another great quality a good student has is being attentive. It is important that not only does a student attend class but pay attention to what his or her professor is teaching and apply the new knowledge. A student who does not pay attention is absent from the class. For example, when I am unable to attend class, I do not get the lesson that was taught for the day. There is no way that I will understand anything that was said in class because I was there to hear it. The same concept applies when a student is absent minded in class and not paying attention to his or her teacher. In order for a student to be successful in his or her class, he or she has to pay attention to what is being taught in his or her class.

Finally, a good student will study. After a student attends his or her class, it is important to study. A student should study so that he or she is fully knowledgeable of the information that was taught. I have always been taught that I should study to show myself approved. The statement I just shared means that I should study to get an understanding of whatever I am studying, and to pass any test on that topic. How can a student be sure of that? A student can set aside time to study a lesson, making sure that he or she understands every aspect of the lesson. A student should also test himself or herself so that he or she knows that he or she understands it. I also think that a student should know his or her study habits and abilities. It may be more helpful to some students to work in study groups. Whatever the method, studying makes a good student.

Being a successful student takes a lot of hard work. There is no easy way around passing a class. The only way to successfully pass a class is by being a good student. Certain qualities good students have to help to pass a class like coming to class on time, paying attention in class, and spending time outside of class testing themselves knowledge of the lesson. These qualities make a good successful student.

***

Why I Like This Essay: I like this essay because this topic on being a good student allows me, as the professor, to help students assess whether they really know how to be good students and how to be self-conscious about the process of becoming better students. Tiara's essay demonstrates that she has taken this introspection seriously and that she knows what she needs to do to be a good student and that she has mastered the basics of being able to articulate these important ideas in traditional essay structure.
Dr. Valerie Dotson, Professor of English

Marriage Is Not for Me

John Pearson
ENGL 0099
♦♦♦

Some people like the idea of pretty dresses, handsome tuxedos, and beautiful receptions. Other people like the idea of spending the rest of their lives with the person that they consider to be their soul mate. And there are even some people who welcome the opportunity to have that person in order to grow closer to God. In my opinion, all of these reasons are highly overrated and give me no motivation to ever want to get married again. The main reasons why I believe that I will never get married again are all the planning that goes into the wedding, losing all of my freedom, and the possibility of another divorce.

One reason why I do not believe I will ever get married again is the wedding planning. Planning a wedding requires a lot of time and money. The wedding planning was quite exhausting to our incomes and our energy. We had to start off by finding a preacher that would agree to perform the wedding ceremony. After the preacher agreed to marry us, he wanted us to participate in marriage counseling. After the marriage counseling, it was time for us to start the major wedding planning. My ex-wife was the type of woman who wanted the traditional church wedding. We had the maid of honor, the groomsmen, the bridesmaids, and of course, the best man. We spent a lot of money on the wedding dress and my tuxedo. The bulk of the money we spent all went on the wedding reception. I never knew that it cost so much to feed 150 people. We also put out a lot of money on the wedding cake. Now that we had everything in place, we had to make sure everyone got to the church on time and that everyone was in place. Getting everyone on the same page for a wedding is very time consuming, and we soon found out that it was very hard to get some people to cooperate. Finally, after people showed up and were put in their proper places, the ceremony was performed. The actual ceremony lasted all of fifteen minutes. I was so glad it was all over because in my opinion a year's worth of planning and several thousand dollars just was not worth the five minutes it took to say "I do."

Another thing I hated about being married was losing my freedom. First off, I already had to see this person every day, and sometimes I just needed a break. I was expected to come home from work at the same time every day. I also would be given a hard time by my wife if I just wanted to go shoot basketball or even go shoot pool with my friends sometimes. It is like she wanted me with her all day every day until she wanted to go do something with her friends. When it came time for her to do something with her friends, I was just supposed to smile and be ok with it. Now that I look back on it, my marriage was one messed up situation. I also hated the fact of having to deal with her different attitudes from day to day. I did not know from one day to the next if I was married to Dr. Jekyll or Mrs. Hyde. One minute she loved me, and the next minute she hated me. One day she was in love with me, and the next day she could not stand to look at me. Putting all this together with sharing bank accounts, the pressure to have children, and the pressure to buy a house was a recipe for disaster. When I look back over the course of the marriage, all of these things started to take place in the first year. I really did want to be married, but the idea of being a kept man, and being rushed into every detail of life turned me off of the idea of being married really fast. The things that I had to endure to be married were not worth it to me. By the way, for those who do not know what a kept man is, it is a man who always does exactly what his wife tells him to do.

The main reason why I believe I will never get married again is the possibility of another divorce. Divorce was very hard for me to deal with. I felt that I had given marriage my all, and getting a divorce just made me feel like I had received nothing in return. All of a sudden, the person I thought I loved with all my heart, I could not even stand the sight of now. After all the arguing and differences of opinion, the day for a divorce had come. Even though I was tired of being with a person that I felt did not really love me anyway, it still did not make the divorce any easier. We did not have any children together in the four and a half years we were married, but she did have a son that I had become very fond of. It was hard being divorced and starting life over on my own, but it was even harder not being able to be in my son's life on a daily basis. His mother was very immature. She started off letting me see my son once a week. After she started a new relationship, she felt that since he was not my biological child that it would be best that I did not see him at all. Of all my negative marital experiences, not being able to see my son crushed me the most. Not being able to see my son not only turned me off of getting married again, but it also made me never want to marry a woman who already has a child again.

I have several reasons why I will never get married again. My reasons go from bad to worse. I do not knock anyone who wants to get married, but it is definitely not for me. From all the wedding planning, to feeling like a prisoner in my own home, to ultimately getting a divorce, my experience being married was a disaster. I feel like I wasted a lot of time and money. The money I can replace, but the time I will never regain. Marriage taught me a lot of things, but the most important thing it taught me is that I enjoy not being married even more. If I ever get married again, it will be an act of God and completely out of my control.

***

Why I Like This Essay: I really enjoyed reading this essay because of the honest and detailed examples that really give readers insight into the sometimes neglected male perspective related to marriage and divorce. John's essay demonstrates how effective and compelling personal experience essays can be when writers are willing to be a bit vulnerable and truly let the reader share in their experiences. This is how the best expository essays are built and how writers can generate interesting, well-developed essays, even in a timed writing environment.
Dr. Valerie Dotson, Professor of English

Compare and Contrast: Two Kinds of Cars

Cassandra Lewis
ENGL 0099

◆◆◆

The Mitsubishi Galant and the Volkswagen Golf differ in many ways, but show similarities in other ways. The cars differ in size, appearance, and cost. Both cars are great for traveling and using for everyday living.

The Mitsubishi Galant has a larger body size than the Volkswagen Golf. Galant cars are larger on the outside, and the trunk space is average. A person wanting to purchase a Galant would think he or she is getting a larger car, but looks are deceiving. The Volkswagen Golf is a smaller car on the outside, but has a larger interior. The front seats of a Volkswagen Golf would fit a person over six feet tall, and weighing over two hundred pounds, which is surprising when looking at the car from the outside. Volkswagen Golfs have a bigger trunk space where one can keep all sorts of items. Both cars are nice in size.

The Mitsubishi Galant and Volkswagen Golf styles are different, but they are both nice cars. The Galant cars were made in Japan and the Volkswagen Golfs were made in Germany. Most people admire the Galant's profile from a distance because it is nice to look at. However, the Galant is a car to look good for years to come; it ages very well, and has a good re-sale value. Volkswagen Golf's are especially nice cars, but they have an outdated look of the old days. These cars will look great for years to come also and hold their value. There are a lot of small things about the Volkswagen Golf that makes it an interesting car. The interior lights are normally blue and red, which makes the car stand out because most cars do not have two different interior lights. The Golf drives well, holds the road nicely, and also has a nice profile.

When purchasing a Volkswagen Golf or Mitsubishi Galant, the pricing is very close. Someone wanting to compare pricing for both cars would spend about $2,000 more for the Mitsubishi Galant than for the Volkswagen Golf. Most people purchase both cars used, but they are still buying great cars. The re-sale value is fairly high. Someone would benefit greatly in purchasing either car. When they compare the Mitsubishi Galant to the Volkswagen Golf, they would find both are great cars, fairly easy to maintain, look great, and have a good re-sale value. The Mitsubishi Galant and Volkswagen Golf differ in size, cost, and appearance, but would be good cars for everyday use and travelling distances.

***

Why I Like This Essay: Cassandra Lewis enrolled in English 0099 in a challenging summer course format. Faced with the pressure of writing timed essays and qualifying for exit testing, she worked diligently on course assignments. Writing a comparison and contrast essay demands good organizational skills, and Cassandra's essay provides a good model of those skills. Using a clear set of criteria to evaluate the Galant and the Golf automobiles, she supports her analysis with interesting details. Acknowledging that consumers care about size, design, and cost, she applies critical thinking to the evaluation process. Although the Galant appears to be larger, she observes that the Golf has more interior space. She also reminds readers about cost differentials. Rewarded for her hard work by successfully completing English 0099, Cassandra is also honored by the publication of her essay in The Polishing Cloth.
Jean Hakes, Instructor of English

Stinker

Desiree' Hines
ENGL 0099

♦♦♦

In my eighteen years of life, I've had several moments of awkwardness and embarrassment that I can recall. Nothing in my life could honestly prepare me for the hurt and shame that I felt one day in sixth grade. Embarrassment was something I could handle back then, but being bullied was not. Because of the emotions and aftermath, I can say this story would have to be the most embarrassing moment in my life.

On that tragic day in sixth grade, the school was having hat day, the day anyone can wear a favorite hat while in school. I decided to wear my lucky tie dye shirt and hat. Before I went to school, I washed up and put plenty of deodorant on. Later on that day, I noticed that a bunch of fellow classmates were snickering behind me and saying something about my clothes. When I went to my sixth period class, the teacher left the room to copy the class assignments. A girl started to chant and tell me in front of the class that I smelled. The whole class except my friend was chanting and calling me "Stinker." I ran out of the classroom and cried.

My emotions through the whole predicament were twisted. I've never been so embarrassed in my life. I can still feel the pain and tears that I shed that day. I honestly didn't know that I smelled until I lifted up my arms and smelled the stench. I had to go to the counselor's office with the girl who started the problem and explain the story.

The aftermath of the story was that I was asked to wash up and go back to class. People in my seventh period class were still giggling and saying mean comments. Not only did I have to endure that, but I had to go home in tears and tell my mom the whole story. I didn't tell my mom until I took my bath and finished my homework that night. My life at that time was not that easy because my family and I had just moved from California. I hardly had any friends, and because of these reasons my self-esteem was low. That event made me very insecure with myself.

What I've learned from this experience is that no matter what I go through, I did and always will, pick myself back up and stay strong. This experience also taught me that hygiene is really important, and from that day on I always bring extra clothes and deodorant with me, at all times. Through life we gain experiences and learn. With that being said, I believe that it's ok to laugh at embarrassing moments. I'm pretty sure there will be plenty more embarrassing moments in the future.

***

Why I Like This Essay: This composition was a response to an assignment asking for a description of an embarrassing moment. What makes it work so well is that it shows (instead of tells) a painful coming-of-age story. Desiree's narrative is so filled with emotional details that her readers cannot help but find themselves right back in the sixth grade as they read this essay.
Shellie Sims-Welch, Instructor of English

What Is the Most Important Thing You Hope to Someday Give Your Children?

Samuel Adeseye
ESL 0091

◆◆◆

He took a few unstable attempts at walking for the first time, but then, he stumbled and fell head-long, bruising his nose during the process. His father with his arms wide open at the other end of the room kept on smiling and beckoning on him with some encouragement gestures. The little boy, not relenting, made more frantic efforts to please his father. At last, he began a goose-like walk, step by step, toward his father. One of the words his father said to him was come on my boy, you deserve this because you have crawled enough. At bed time when his father was reflecting on the scenario that took place during the noon time of that day, he also looked ahead toward the future of his little boy and said in his mind, "I will one day relate what happened today to this boy, and I will let him know that life is a process; everyone has to crawl before walking." The most important thing I hope to someday give my children is to teach them the legacy of following the due processes of life and never think that there is ever a short-cut to success in life. I will also do everything possible to ensure that they are well educated.

To start with, in the words of a wide man, "men are in sizes and life is in phases." I believe that there is no short-cut to success in life and this is the most important legacy I wish to leave my children with. I will start to teach my children from their early lives that life is like a building which needs proper planning and a sequential pattern of execution; step by step, from the foundation before it will eventually stand up as a habitable edifice. Like the father of the little boy at the other end of the room, I will continue to advise, guide, and encourage my children to embrace the principle of leaping before jumping. I will let them understand that Rome was not built in a day, and to be successful in life, they have to pay their dues of working hard, doing the right things and doing what is needed to be done per time, and most importantly, be patient and never be in a do or die attitude of succeeding at all cost.

In addition to giving them the legacy of following the due processes of life by ensuring that they always crawl before walking, I will do everything within my capacity to ensure that they are all well educated. I know that education is the road map to liberty and success as opined and confirmed by Dr. Ben Carson's life. Without good education, Obama an never think of planning to vie for the position of the presidency and dream of becoming one today.

In order to wrap up this piece, the most important legacy I live by and would hope to give to my children is the attitude of following the due processes of life without ending to cut corners. Although I know that education is one of the greatest legacies that can be bequeathed to one's children, I believe it is not enough as there are many educational bigots in the society out there doing more harm to life than good. Besides, education is not enough to make anyone successful. There are some basic principles of life like following the due processes of life, as I have tried to point out in this essay, that are more important in making a complete human entity. As a result, because I do not want my children to only be successful, but be a complete and whole entity, the most important legacy I hope to someday leave them is understanding the due processes of life!

The Best 1,850 Pesos Ever Spent

Adam Stern
ENGL 1101
♦♦♦

"The cabin door has now been shut and we will be in the air on our way to Santo Domingo, Dominican Republic very shortly," a flight attendant informed the passengers of flight 783 as we began to embark. I had flown countless times to places all over the country, experiencing what American living was like in places such as New York, Chicago, Las Vegas and Hawaii, but that flight last summer took me to experience a sort of travel I had never before experienced: international travel.

Since childhood, I had always been intrigued by cultures and languages of countries other than my own. Having grown up in Los Angeles, many of my friends were Mexican and spoke Spanish. My two best friends were brothers, Jose and Pedro, who lived three houses down from mine. Their home always had a delicious smell of warm, home-made corn tortillas and fresh tomato salsa. The walls of the living room were adorned with typical wall hangings from their native country, bright colors on these things that resembled blankets. Spanish soap operas would be blaring in the background as the three of us would play with our dozens of Matchbox cars on the cold tan tile. This mini-culture living just a few houses down absolutely fascinated me and I was so hungry to learn more and more about their culture and their language. Their mother taught me Spanish words here and there. She explained to me that if I took Spanish classes in school, the teacher would not only teach the Spanish language, but also teach about the cultures associated with that language throughout the world. To say the least, I enrolled in the first Spanish class I could and continued my Spanish studies all through my school career. Before I knew it, I was graduating high school, essentially fluent in Spanish, and starving to visit a Spanish speaking country to put all that I had learned to the test.

When I was 19, I started working with a youth empowerment based non-profit organization. This organization hosted workshops and camps around the world teaching methods of how to live positively, successfully, and happily. This quickly became my dream job. After several years of working with this organization, I was asked if I would be willing to travel to the Dominican Republic to teach entrepreneurship to thirty Dominican students. Without hesitation, I said I would. Three months later, I found myself boarding a plane to the Dominican Republic. I knew this was going to be an eye-opening experience for me. I simply couldn't wait to learn about the culture of this country first-hand and get that first stamp on the eighth page of my passport.

"Please close your tray tables, return your seats to the upright position, and store all belongings. We are now making our final descent..." notified the flight attendant in a muffled voice. We finally landed on a runway that seemed smaller than the driveways of most American homes, and I could hardly wait to get off the plane to see all of the advertisements and signs in Spanish, to really 'dig my teeth' into this foreign culture. After walking through the terminal of the tiny airport taking in all of the excitement and sights, I finally made it to baggage claim where I met up with my native co-worker, Ruth.

After a long car ride into the city, we arrived at our impressively large hotel in the heart of Santo Domingo, 'The capital city' as the locals call it. The front desk of the hotel acted not only as a typical front desk of a hotel, but also as a mini-bank where you could exchange American dollars for Dominican pesos. "37/1 Exchange Rate" a sign read behind the hotel staff at the tan colored marble desk. "While I'm here," I thought to myself, "I might as well exchange some money." There, I exchanged $50 worth of American dollars into pesos, and was soon the proud carrier of 1,850 Dominican pesos.

During the day, we taught the students at the local college. Then, I switched hats from instructor to tourist to explore the sights, tastes, and sounds of the capital city in the evenings. Ruth was an excellent tour guide, proudly showing me around her home country. She took me to historic sites and explained how business and education worked. She told stories about how the country was formed through anecdotes that sounded similar to those told about America and gave me real hands-on learning about the culture of this fascinating island.

One afternoon, one of our students brought us to a local orphanage where she volunteers. We toured the small facility that 83 girls, ages 8-14, called home. We were shown where the girls sleep: 15-20 girls in a room no bigger than 600 square feet in bunk beds, like a scene straight out of the movie *Annie*. We were brought to the poorly-lit and cramped dining hall to experience what a typical dinner was like for them. Just off the dining hall was the kitchen where the food was prepared. In a large, cast-iron 15-gallon kettle, black beans were being stewed and just next to it, a slightly larger kettle overflowed with white rice. I was disheartened to learn that this was a typical dinner for them and that roughly 185 pesos, or five US dollars, was the painfully low budget for dinner to feed all 83 hungry mouths. I was also informed that at times, their volunteer staff is forced to go to the local market to beg for donations of rice and beans to feed the girls. After dinner, we really formed a connection with the girls as we played with them for a few hours in their play yard, a yard that was mainly dirt with very little grass. Even though the girls were not living in the most desirable of conditions, they were so thankful to have food in their stomachs, clothes on their body, and a bed to sleep in at night. Their spirit and the attitude of gratitude they possessed astounded me. They didn't have much, but were happy with what they did have. As the sun began to set, and after being almost eaten alive by mosquitoes, we decided it was time to head back to the hotel. We said our goodbyes and with outstretched arms, the girls gave us almost a million hugs. We were led out by one of the volunteers of the home and I couldn't help but wonder how I could do something to help these girls. I suddenly remembered I had exchanged some American dollars into pesos earlier in the week. I knew that if I gave the home what I had, I could provide dinner for the girls for over a week. I immediately pulled out my wallet, walked over to the volunteer, handed her 1,850 pesos and told her that I wanted to contribute something to these girls. She let out a huge smile and gave me one of the most meaningful hugs I've ever been given. Fifty dollars was a lot of money to simply give away, but knowing that my small contribution could feed the eighty three girls for over a week made it arguably the best $50 I have ever spent.

I had always dreamed of visiting a foreign country, a country where I could practice the language I had been learning virtually my entire life. I was finally given this opportunity I had always desired and embraced it. I traveled to the Dominican Republic with the expectations that I would learn about the culture of this country first hand. When the trip finally ended, I accomplished what I came to do. What I didn't expect, was the incredible lesson I learned about gratitude and appreciation. It's safe to say that the life I live is significantly more luxurious than that of the girls at that orphanage in Santo Domingo. I may not drive an expensive sports car or be as financially independent as I would like to be, but I am fortunate enough that I don't have to resort to eating rice and beans every night for dinner and have the luxury of going to bed each night in my own room. I learned a lesson on this trip that is sure to stick with me for the rest of my life. I can now say that I live my life focusing on the incredible things I do have, not the things I don't and for this lesson, I am truly grateful.

***

Why I Like This Essay: Adam Stern's essay is not only an excellent and well organized example of a successfully written piece, but also a heartwarming retelling of a meaningful experience that moves readers to contemplate their place in the world. In my English 1101 classes, students' first assignment is to write about an experience that provided them with personal insight. Adam's essay begins with the tantalizing title, "The Best 1850 Ever Spent." He develops the retelling of his experiences on a trip to the Dominican Republic drawing in his readers with an effective flashback and then blending background information and narration with colorful dialogue and description as he reveals how his experience running a youth camp led him to a realization that changed his life. Adam is not only a great storyteller, but a man whose personal message resonates with all who read his essay.

Beverly Santillo, Assistant Professor of English

Changing Woman

Chachee Valentine
ENGL 1101

♦♦♦

"Maggie! Maggie!" The echo of his cry boomeranged off the reservoir walls of Abiquiu Lake. There I sat siphoning air off the desert landscape, taking in the majestic beauty of northern New Mexico. For three long nights I had sobbed myself to sleep. Grieving alone, I received counsel from Pedernal, quite possibly the most mysterious, intoxicating mesa in the Southwest. According to locals, the Native Americans call the mountain, "Changing Woman." I have no idea whether this namesake is true, but there is a truth about the comfort of Pedernal that resonates inside of me.

High on my perch overlooking the lake, my inner peace was interrupted by the call of a woman's name and a big splash. Barefoot, and with no time to think, I jumped from my favorite boulder overlooking the lake below, and with a whoosh of adrenaline, I scurried across rock, shards of fish bones, and broken beer-bottle glass until I reached the rickety, wooden dock.

The man ahead barely looked me in the eyes, but I could sense his plea to help his Maggie, who had slipped off the dock while casting her line. As he called out to Maggie again, I flew past him as if flaunting a cape and dove in. My hands cupped the water making a direct path to Maggie who did not know how to swim. Her mouth was gaping in the shape of panic, gasping for air like a sunny out of water under the heat of the August sun. Maggie's arms flapped, and her loose skin bubbled on the water like raw bacon hitting a hot skillet. Maggie's fear of drowning was creating a whirlpool around us. "Don't drown me, Maggie," I said, as I wrapped my right arm around her sagging neck.

Swimming for two moved us in slow motion. Maggie's sweetheart was pacing as we climbed on dock. "My sweetheart, everything is fine," Maggie told him, as if soothing a small child.

For days I replayed those words to myself because they made me smile, as if something told me one day my heart would be full.

It is true what people say about time standing still when faced with a dire situation. There was a moment in the chilly water when I doubted my ability to get Maggie and me safely back to the dock. That uncertainty propelled me to think random, absurd thoughts, like eating pineapple pizza. Carving our way through Abiquiu Lake, I thought to myself that upon my return to Atlanta, I would eat pineapple pizza from Fellini's, which I did. With every bite of pineapple I remembered the sun's glare in my eyes that day at the lake, and every doughy swallow of pizza crust symbolized my big toe stubbing red rock, while my hand squeezed Maggie's hand to not let go as I dragged her to higher ground.

After going through their lunch box and finding kiddie cups of apple juice, I noticed that Maggie's sweetheart was bleeding from a fishing hook anchored to his forearm. Pulling back the foils on their juices, I asked them to drink up while motioning to him about the hook. Numb from the experience, the poor guy had not even noticed his injury. He knocked back his juice and waved me away like a fly as I plucked the hook from his taut skin. Clearly, his focus was still on Maggie.

Four months before the experience at Pedernal, I had broken up with my family. We did not have a fight, and I did not pick and choose relatives with whom I would stay in touch. Breaking up with my family meant saying good-bye to everyone. While it would be too much to explain why I chose this drastic direction for my life, I will say that my decision was healthy and still reigns as the best gift I have ever given to myself. On the day I was attempting to secure inner peace at Abiquiu Lake, I knew I had a lot to heal; still do. Back when I dove into Abiquiu Lake to help Maggie, New Mexico had become for me, like so many others, a place for healing. Some people believe the healing qualities of New Mexico have to do with the volcanic rock. Others say it is the bloody history between the Spanish and the Native Americans. It might be both.

Though I did not, and do not, regret my choice to leave my blood relations, that day at the lake I was experiencing loss, but more than a single loss. The day my life crossed with

Maggie in the choppy lake, I was feeling the loss of a loss: a silent death. For as long as I can remember, I had grown up feeling disconnected from my relatives (my disconnect from them, and their disconnect from me and from each other). We were never a unit, but rather separate pieces to a puzzle that did not fit.

That afternoon, I sat on the rocks thinking, meditating, and praying. Not only was I grieving for the faces of family I would never see again, I grieved for the loss of my own face, the familiar face with whom I had gone through so much. My eyes that looked back at me whenever I was in the presence of my family would never again reflect their blanket of sadness. Even though it was a moment I had been waiting for my entire life, the sorrow I felt was palpable. The sick comfort I had always hid behind or returned to like an abusive lover was leaving me and I felt lost.

Waving good-bye to their taillights as they faded into the burnt-orange dusk, I wondered: Did some unknown higher power place me at Abiquiu Lake to save Maggie's life, or was I the one who needed saving that day, and was Maggie sent to the lake for me? Though I will never know who was saving whom that day, it is a mystery I love to explore. One thing I cannot deny is that the moment I dove into Abiquiu Lake to swim for Maggie, I felt a purpose. Aware of my own life force, I learned how my electrical current keeps me moving forward, and how my will to live directs my journey and nothing else.

On the plane back home I thought about "Changing Woman," and all the years I had been drawn to her presence. What the mountain reflects back to me about her tumultuous history, the bloodshed, her indescribable beauty, is synonymous with my path, and the changes I have weathered. It is the sweetest lullaby that still haunts me in a whisper when I dream. "My sweetheart, everything is fine."

***

Why I Like This Essay: Chachee's essay is written well enough to go in a memoir. The brilliance of the essay is in balancing the narrative elements with the philosophical rumination. Writing a narrative essay is not hard but it is hard to do well and she knows how to use description, vocabulary, dialogue, action, and intrigue to create a space of intimacy and leave the reader feeling changed. As she describes how she was changed I am reminded of the times in my life that have transformed me - for good or bad. This essay was the first, and for me, the most vulnerable of the four essays she wrote for me during the semester. I hope you enjoy it as much as I do.
Deanna Clark, Instructor of English

Comparing College Education in Ghana and That of the United States of America: University of Ghana and Georgia State University

Richard Abdulai
ENGL 1101

An academic revolution and transformation has taken place in higher education for the past few decades. Arguably, the changes in the recent trend of higher education are more dramatic than before. According to the 1998 UNESCO world conference on higher education report, the academic changes of the late 20th and early 21st centuries are more extensive due to their global nature and the number of institutions and people they affect. Recent trends in higher education have witnessed an increase in students studying abroad. This global trend in higher education has greatly impacted universities to a point that studies are no longer limited by national boundaries. Some of the oldest and most prestigious universities such as Cambridge, Harvard, and Oxford, have been able to stand the test of time. A study conducted by the World Bank indicates that new universities can also grow into top quality institutions when the necessary resources are made available to them. The University of Ghana and Georgia State University are similar great institutions of our time. The geographical location of both universities, their organizational structure, facilities, style, and methods of teaching set these two educational institutions apart, yet they are closely related.

First and foremost, one striking difference between the two schools can be derived from their names. Georgia State University from its name is a state funded school, while the University of Ghana, on the other hand, is funded by the government of Ghana. However, there are similarities between both schools that cannot be overlooked. For example, both universities have beautifully built websites that give a detailed history of each university. The "About" page of the University of Ghana, for example, describes and gives detailed information about the purpose behind building the school. Furthermore, it includes statistics on its graduation and enrollment, its associations and links, and its institutional affiliations. In addition, it provides detailed descriptions of its colleges, which include: College of Health Sciences, which has a medical, dental, allied health services, public health, and nursing school; the College of Agriculture and Consumer Sciences, with a school of agriculture and a research center, as well as arts, law, science, business and engineering divisions; and also describes Research Institutes. These institutes include the Institute of African Studies; the Institute of Adult Education; the Institute of Statistical, Social and Economic Research; the Memorial Institute for Medical Research; and the Institute for Population Studies. Furthermore, the "About" page also gives insight as to the research and learning centers, and states that it works with 17 of such learning centers or libraries.

Though both universities have an "About" page, there is a difference between the structure and the content of both institutions' websites. For example, on Georgia State's website, the President includes a "Welcome" message, which is quite characteristic for a university in the United States. The website also includes a mission statement, and several other facts about Georgia State, including an overview of its structure, its schools, tuition rates, and research centers, while the University of Ghana's website has little or no information about tuition rates, research centers and an overview of the institution's structure.

There is yet another difference here with the two universities in addition to, of course, the substances of their "About" messages, and the differences in the schools and the divisions of each university. This difference is the declaration by Georgia State of its financial assets in a paragraph on the "About" page. The "About" pages above were referenced because they are quite useful in pinpointing general similarities, and especially differences, in the two institutions. For example, from these pages it was found that whereas Georgia State is a research university and serves around 30,000 students, the University of Ghana, though with around the same number of students, is one of the largest and most prestigious universities in Africa. This, then, shows various trends with regards to education. Though both universities have a research focus, especially in the medical field, and both have around the same number of students, the goal and specifics? of each is very different, and these range from the way things are taught and the actual curriculum, to the various fields where emphasis is most placed (i.e. research at Georgia State, and the medical field at the University of Ghana). These statistics also show that perhaps the situation in Africa does not so much stress education, for the Georgia State research institution is truly quite small for the United States.

Furthermore, both institutions are into higher learning; Georgia State University is equipped with modern and more advance facilities compare to that of the University of Ghana. The school has well stuffed libraries for research work, a research center for various fields of study, and computer laboratories. The University of Ghana, on the other hand, lacks most of these learning facilities. The majority of students do not even have access to computers. Libraries are not well stuffed. Surprisingly, you can find over three hundred students in a lecture room with one instructor. These in most at times do not create a good environment for effective studies.

Another major difference between these two institutions is the flexibility students enjoy at Georgia State University. Students at Georgia State have the opportunity to choose from the various lecture hours to suit their schedules. This kind of flexibility does not exist at University of Ghana. Students of University of Ghana have to attend lectures at a particular time of the day. This does not give room for flexibility. It is therefore impossible to work or get involved in other activities apart from schooling.

According to paragraphs above, there are many similarities and differences between the University of Ghana and Georgia State University. Though this paper has illustrated many more differences, its thesis has sought to also see whether either institution is better suited, and what this may mean, and has instead found that both institution are well-qualified to instruct the students, and that neither can take the lead, for both countries in which they exist are different. Thus, education in one country will be different from that in another country, and it is important to recognize this fact in order to allow for these differences to be adequately addressed by the education systems in any country.

***

Why I Like This Essay: Despite struggling with sentence-level errors in early drafts of this essay, the student ultimately develops a thoughtful comparison of the two universities. Comparisons are developed with clear, specific details. In addition to providing adequate development for the comparison, the student avoids a "so what" thesis; this means that the student opens up the topic, contextualizes it. The introduction and conclusion reiterate the importance of the topic (higher education), as well as the importance of careful analysis when comparing educational institutions in different countries.
Amber Brooks, Instructor of English

Facebook Friendships

Courtney Linden
ENGL 1101

Almost everyone and everything has a Facebook page. These people all check their status and update their posts on an almost hourly basis. There are definite benefits to Facebook membership, such as self publicity and advertising. These benefits are especially important for non-personal relations such as businesses and news broadcasts. There are, however, clear issues developing with Facebook and friendship. Gone are the days when letters and phone calls were how people stayed in touch. Brief, electronic communication has taken over completely, and it has become damaging to healthy relationships. Facebook friendships are not a healthy way of maintaining correspondence. These friendships encourage poor grammar, inhibit personal privacy, and limit personal, one-on-one relationships. Through these online friendships, people are actually growing farther apart in a time when communication has become so much easier.

Society today is rampant with poor grammar. It can be seen on billboards like "DNT TXT N DRV" and even in school papers. The other day in my English class, my professor, a lovely Miss Shelfer, discussed some errors on the class's diagnostic essays. I was appalled to hear that a student had included "U" in replacement of "You." This shortening of words is greatly encouraged by Facebook relationships as it limits the amount of text one can put up especially on cell phones. The constant and yet limiting access encourages users to shorten their statements to quickly get their point across. Another example of Facebook encouraging poor grammar is hearing phrases such as "LOL" and "WTF" in normal conversation. Acronyms are not actual words, and yet people use them rather than clearly expressing themselves, thus limiting their use of proper grammar and effective vocabulary. True emotions cannot be expressed in three letter acronyms. This kind of shortening of words and text-speak also limits people's vocabulary. I was recently having a conversation with a college graduate who happens to be a Facebook addict. This individual is seemingly intelligent, but throughout our conversation, she consistently used words improperly. She spoke of a "precociously" balanced object and of her "tillative" plans. I asked her what she meant and if she knew the words she had just used. The college graduate giggled and said something along the lines of being more used to Facebook typing and having it edited for her. I couldn't help but roll my eyes and think how odd her conversations on Facebook must be with so many erroneous words in them.

I treasure my privacy. As the youngest girl in a family of all boys, being able to have a room to myself was a total blessing. Having freedom of personal space and allotted total privacy helped me feel comfortable and happy. I enjoy keeping my private life private and sharing certain things with certain people. Facebook friendships, however, have a complete lack of personal privacy. Everything is streamed online for any Facebook friends to view, and this public information can be very detrimental to relationships. People can jump to conclusions, and the lack of privacy in their conversations can lead to serious misunderstandings. I have been privy to an argument between two of my close friends, an argument that was blown way out of proportion because every aspect of their dispute was broadcast publicly on Facebook. My friend Tim had been casually dating a girl named Marnie. Marnie was also a good friend of Tim's buddy Adam and ended up going to a concert with Adam. Adam and Marnie both posted on their Facebook pages that they were out together. The concert was merely a friendly venture without Tim since he had no desire to go and did not enjoy the music style that Adam and Marnie did. Having seen the public post on Facebook, Tim became infuriated and vengefully jealous. Tim proceeded to post derogatory statements about Marnie and her alleged promiscuity. In addition, he accused Adam of being a backstabber. This public forum was no place for this kind of discussion. The conversation escalated to several secrets and accusations being broadcast on Facebook. Ultimately the demise in Tim and Adam's friendship can be directly attributed to Facebook's lack of privacy in communications. Had Tim, Marnie and Adam discussed the situation in person or kept it private until they could all talk, the truth of the matter would probably have been clearer to Tim. Relationships, for many, are also a private matter. Some people, though, have developed a need for public validation in their relationship. One such instance happened to my friend Mark. Mark is a professional photographer and has used Facebook primarily as a form of self-publicity. He began dating a girl who was also a friend of his on Facebook. Mark's Facebook was regularly being updated with blogs about photography or new photos, but nothing personal was publicized. This girl began to feel insecure about their relationship because he never posted anything about her, and he hadn't changed his relationship status. Mark insisted that he was using Facebook solely for business and wanted to keep their relationship out of a public forum. This girl had become so dependent on the image portrayed on Facebook that she simply could not fathom his not wanting everything to be broadcast. Her insistence upon public validation and his inability to understand it quickly led to their breakup. Privacy should be allowed to anyone who so desires it, but because of Facebook's public forums, privacy is not always the case.

Relationships are damaged by Facebook pages in many ways. There was once a time when getting butterflies in one's stomach when receiving correspondence via post was a commonly shared experience among most people. Sitting down for a lunch with a friend after a long separation and catching up on missed events was an absolute pleasure and a sign of a close friendship. These one-on-one relationships are dwindling and have been taken over by electronic online socializing. I have personally missed out on social events because people do not think to call or send an invitation. For example, I have an old group of friends who have monthly barbeques. Not long ago, I ran into a few of these friends and was asked why I no longer attend these cookouts. I was confused by the question because I assumed the functions no longer happened since I did not get any phone calls to invite me. My friends were amused by my confusion and let me know that the invites were posted on Facebook and that I would need to get one in order to be aware of the barbeques. I felt offended that my presence was only deemed appropriate if I had received the invite via Facebook. Another example of Facebook's damaging personal relationships is the inability to stay in touch with people without the site as an intermediary. I have lived in nine different states. Moving around has made it so that I have many people I once corresponded with through letters. The letters were always hand written and accompanied by a photo. Suddenly, as Facebook popped up, my mailbox became emptier. I no longer get the letters I used to from my friends around the country. I often send friends greeting cards and get no response anymore. Most of my long distance friends have said that they keep in touch via Facebook, and without an account, I am out of touch. This lack of personal communication ties directly into the use of Facebook as a sole method of interaction.

The inability for people to meet one-on-one and communicate through traditional methods grows stronger with every Facebook page created. Facebook has invited people to dumb down their language for public display. People's lives, both social and emotional, are now controlled by their online status. Facebook friendships are not a healthy way of maintaining correspondence. Facebook is merely one facet of the ever-growing trend in social media that enables people to simultaneously isolate themselves while validating their existence through a few keystrokes, however misspelled or grammatically incorrect that validation may be.

***

Why I Like This Essay: Courtney's essay has a very clear thesis, which she develops with specific and personal examples. Her writing is natural and concise and resonated with me and, I think, with any reader because it obviously comes from the personal experience of a person who thinks deeply about her environment and the effects of trends and social media on that environment.
Mary Shelfer, Instructor of English

Connecting the Dots

Eduardo Jaen Diez
ENGL 1101

Just a few years ago, when I was working and I had money to spend, I never thought about going back to school. After working in my job designing maps for almost five years, I realized that I could not move forward in life without a degree. Although it can be very difficult returning to school later in life, I knew it would have a huge impact on my future. Not only would studying advance my career, but also it would be the best way to improve myself. Since I decided to go back to school, I have become a much better critical thinker, and I have developed new interests and have new goals.

I used to hate reading books before going back to school because I was not able to fully understand the ideas within the texts. Now because I have to read many books, articles, and reviews for many of my classes, I can clearly see how wrong I was. Moreover, studying in another language has created a strong desire to expand my knowledge and challenge myself to try to improve and to advance my critical thinking skills. Thanks to many teachers who have encouraged me to read, I have a much clearer idea about how to find new alternatives in order to solve problems in my daily life. Due to the books that I read for my philosophy class, I can see how the philosopher's ideas are still related to today's society.

Going back to school after being out for almost five years has improved my critical thinking skills. This is a very useful skill that I am learning because it gives me a crucial tool to better evaluate problems. It is a priceless skill that helps me decide the best available options, opinions, and ways for me when there are several alternatives to choose from.

Acquiring new interests has also been among the several benefits that going back to school has helped me develop. Before starting again in school, my mind was so narrow that I was not aware of how many interesting things were around me. The most important result of my return to school was without any doubt the broadening of my mind. For instance, at that time when I started facing new challenges that I had to overcome, English was the hardest one on my list. The first English course that I took was very difficult and frustrating because I could not see any possible application. In the end, all the hard work that was required paid off when I went abroad for the first time. I was in Malta for almost three weeks and there I started to see how important learning another language was because it helped me to obtain new knowledge. Also, I met new people from different cultures that I previously knew nothing about.

Going back to school helped me to open my eyes because before I did not have a clear idea in my mind about where I wanted to go with my career. I had a great lack of motivation because I did not have any kind of goal to achieve. Once I began to study and saw how many possibilities there were, I started to create new ambitions for my future. At first, the goals that I wanted to achieve were small but in a short period of time they became bigger. I could feel inside me a strong desire to become the best that I could be. One day after class when there were only a few more days until the end of the semester, I stopped by my math teacher´s office to ask her if she thought I was ready to study for an industrial engineering degree. She told me that I was but that I needed to be ready for the high competition in that field. Since then I have been working as hard as I can in order to achieve my goal. Looking back five years ago I could not even imagine that I was capable of studying for a difficult degree in a foreign country. According to Steve Jobs, "again, you can't connect the dots looking forward. You can only connect them looking backwards, so you have to trust that the dots will somehow connect in your future."

Returning to school at a late age was very difficult for me. There is not a day in which I do not regret the step that I took a few years ago when I quit school and began working in a boring job making little money. It is never too late to try again something that you gave up years earlier because perhaps you did not have enough determination or lacked motivation. Now I cannot thank enough the teachers who helped me out and opened my eyes in a time when I was so lost in my life. Going back to school was the best second opportunity that I have ever had in my life.

***

Why I Like This Essay: Eduardo Jaen Diez's "Connecting the Dots" is an educator's dream come true—an essay that humbly expresses gratitude for learning. Diez illustrates this gratitude through personal anecdotes, both from his life and from his time at GPC. He captures the determined spirit of many students here at GPC by recounting his struggles with learning English and with returning to school late in life. At the heart of this essay is a powerfully inspirational message—education is life changing and should be pursued, no matter one's age or life situation.
Alicia Guarracino, Instructor of English

My First Cruise

Vincent E. McQueen
ENGL 1101
♦♦♦

The leviathan lay ahead of me as I came out of the port tunnel to board for my first official cruise on a luxury liner. It was the fall of 2006 and I was looking out at the gargantuan masterpiece of a ship by Carnival. It was blanketed in a rainbow of colors splashed against the white background of its main body. The humongous links in the anchor chain were as large as a Volkswagen and remained still as the choppy gray waters seemed to pummel the bottom of the ship. I can only attempt to take people on this journey with me as I describe what I felt as I embarked on this, one of my lifelong goals, as it had finally arrived.

I eagerly walked through the elevated walkway, feeling the plush carpet beneath my feet and noticed how new it smelled. As I continued up and up and up through the catwalk, I was simply in awe at just how big this ship was. Finally, I was greeted by the smiling staff, professionally dressed in the traditional white tops and black trousers who aided me in finding my cabin. Since I consider myself a connoisseur of coffee, I immediately noticed the intoxicating aroma of various blends as I boarded and knew instantly that I was going to enjoy myself. I decided that as soon as I got settled, I must have a cup. It became an everyday (and sometimes several times a day) occurrence for my cabin attendants.

Not long after reaching my cabin, I heard the signature blaring of the "all aboard" horn. Not only did it sound as if several trains were driving through my head from ear to ear, but I could also feel the vibrations in my bones. I raced to the top rail, as did many of the patrons and saw the crowd of family, friends, and onlookers waving and sending us off. I remembered thinking that they really did look like ants from up there, another testament of the size of the ship. I smelled the saltwater as it dashed against the bow of the bottom of the ship and could actually taste the saltiness in the air. I stood there and watched the port as it got smaller and smaller until it disappeared altogether.

Well, I made my way back to the inside of the ship and as the tangy, saltwater smell was replaced with the pleasant aroma of beef, potatoes, coffee, and new carpet smells, the inside of the ship was immaculately adorned with wood-grain finish on the walls, gargantuan chandeliers hanging from the ceilings, traditional and life-like paintings adorning the walls of various landscapes from lush, green mountaintop views to exquisitely-detailed lighthouses surrounded by crashing waves and jagged rocks. I began to familiarize myself with the layout of the huge ship. Although it was loud with the different chatter from the many cruisers, it was a joyous chatter, filled with laughter, singing, and overall excitement.

I made my way to the upper decks and saw the rear engine jutting up from near the rear of the ship. It was massive, at least as wide as a Giant Redwood from California so I ventured toward it to view the rear of the ship and on my way there, some people were already splashing away in the pool, and to my amazement, a giant chess game was underway. This fascinated me not only because I have always wanted to learn how to play chess, but seeing the life-size pieces being moved by the competitors really put it in perspective for me. I stood there for about an hour noticing the knight-to-bishop moves along the white and black checker-painted floor on which they were positioned and remembered I was on my tour of the ship. I reached the back of the ship and even though I could not see the giant propellers spinning, I could see the result. It left a trail of churning water in about a twenty foot wide straight path directly behind the ship. White seagulls shadowed the ship and occasionally dived into the ocean on either side of us. Someone noticed a black whale surfacing and blowing water from the hole in the top of its body and I attempted to snap a photo with my cell phone but as quickly as it surfaced, it was gone.

By that time it was time to go to dinner and there was a certain protocol to follow. They preferred you to dress in dinner attire so I always had on at the least blue or black slacks, a Van Hausen or other button down shirt and tie or a full two-piece suit. The dining hall was exquisite, with fine china and crystal glassware. There were live bands of the traditional ballroom genre, horns, piano concertos, and balladeers. The food tasted totally delicious, my steaks well done, chicken baked to perfection, falling off the bone, vegetables steamed just right with the white rice and green beans looking as if they were painted on the plate. Each meal was even more delightful than the next.

One night, I decided to try out the nightclub that was onboard. There was one which had a jazz-like ambiance as you entered the room, soft music which spoke to you in a delicate almost teasing melody with casual conversations occasionally in the background. I ventured about twenty feet down the hallway and heard and felt the base of the various hip-hop and rock mixes. As I made my way past the packed, raucous-filled room, one not so young lady was atop the table moving to the beat, amazingly keeping her balance in the high heels she had on. How do they do that? I spent a couple hours there dancing and mingling and decided I wanted to go up to the top deck to see the view at night and was astonished as I reached the end of the ship, which by now had become one of my favorite spots to go. The full moon was shining directly in the center of the rear of the boat and threw a double lane of brilliance off the surface of the water which looked like a roadway of light. It was fascinating! The night air was clear and crisp but comfortable with a slight breeze. I retired to my cabin and immediately ordered my nightly coffee, of course, and said, "Wow, I've got to do this more often!"

***

Why I Like This Essay: "My First Cruise" has two factors in its favor beyond meeting the usual requirements of a college-level essay. First, it has a steady narrative and descriptive hand. We are led logically and sequentially through the key parts of that strange animal called a cruise ship without ever feeling like we've veered off course; the essay is detailed, but what's more, it's detailed in all the right ways for a "first" experience. Second, the author places himself front and center in the proceedings. The essay is not just a rote description but a nuanced evocation of this experience; it goes way beyond competence and renders significance.

Michael Diebert, Associate Professor of English

Gimmie an F!

Tan-Phu Lee
ENGL 1101

♦♦♦

When I drive north on Interstate 85 through Duluth, I see a Fry's Electronics retail store to the left of the Lawrenceville exit. At that moment, my heart starts to flutter, and all of these memories come rushing back to me. I picture the polished marble flooring with the grand piano at the entrance. My feet start to ache remembering all of the hours they had to stand and all of the heavy lifting they had to endure. I smell the burnt heat from the shrink wrapping machine. The inane employee pep rallies and the resulting sounds of cheering to the letters in the company name come to mind. "Gimme an F! Gimme an R! Gimme a Y! Gimmie an Apostrophe! Gimme an S!" Just the recollection of the retail experience makes my skin crawl as if I'm watching open-heart surgery. Although I do have amusing and enjoyable memories from working in the retail industry, working at Fry's Electronics as a salesperson was my absolute worst job.

Working in the retail industry is more physically demanding than one would expect. The Fry's Electronics store was over a hundred thousand square feet, and my feet felt like it walked every square inch of that store for nine grueling hours a day, five somber days a week. My body was in constant frantic motion just trying to keep up with the demands of restocking products on row after row of institutional gray aluminum shelving. I must have lifted the weight of the world in randomly labeled boxes from every electronic manufacturer throughout Asia. This paradise of a work environment rewarded me with bunions the size of golf balls and a diagnosis of neuroma. Neuroma is a vicious ailment that rewards its victims with swelling of the nerves throughout the feet such that just taking a step can feel like walking across broken glass. Neuroma has managed to stay with me longer than Lyme disease, leaving me with a life of bunions, hammer toes, and heel spurs.

Upon further reflection, working retail did teach me the life skill of coping with the myriad of people that like to shop at large discount electronics stores located in vast suburban areas. Needless to say, Fry's Electronics attracted a broad spectrum of personalities ranging from the clueless, smartphone-carrying soccer mom to the male nineteen year old junior college student who makes a lifestyle choice to live in their parent's basement while playing fantasy video games for forty-eight hours straight, gaining sustenance from caffeinated sodas and pizza rolls. Yet none of those were as fun to deal with as the customer the employees labeled as "Vocals." Vocals were typically the person, who showed up hours after the store opened, still wiping the fast food crumbs off their shirt, and demanding the plasma television advertised at fifty percent off. Of course, they never noticed the fine print in copy the size of a gnat which read, "While supplies last." Having been blessed with a meteoric rise through the ranks of the Fry's Electronics hierarchy, I was the manager routinely tasked with dealing with the Vocals when the store ran out of inventory on the sale items. Aside from the food crumbs, Vocals were categorized by their consistent arguments. Their argument typically followed the pattern of stating how they drove hours through driving rain that would make Noah cringe.

I remember a time when this argument fell on my deaf ears. I was then greeted in an even louder tone, accompanied by a large determined step into my personal space, claiming Fry's Electronics engaged in the "bait-and-switch" tactic. Given my ignorance, I thought this classically American idiom meant an item was a great bargain—based on "switching" to low prices to "bait" customers to purchase it. So, like a cheap bobble-head doll available on aisle ten, I stood there innocently nodding by head in agreement. To this day, I remain amazed that security did not have to escort the person out of the store. Their rant went on as long as a Congressional filibuster; and while never violent, it did leave me with a craving French fries as the smell on their breath was all I could smell. I'll never make that "bait-and-switch" misunderstanding again.

For the usual customers, those with no really discernible characteristic other than a deep love for anything with a microchip or circuit board, there was still one unifying characteristic. That characteristic was the heartfelt belief that they were funny and original. I do not mean just funny in a tipsy office Christmas party sort of way, but in a way suggesting that they would be opening for Chris Rock on his next tour or winning open microphone night at the local comedy theater. Their best line generally involved responding to my friendly inquiry, "Can I help you with something?" The most common responses were "Yeah, finding the winning lottery ticket." and "Getting me a beautiful woman." People's willingness to be inappropriate in a pseudo-social situation continues to amaze me to this day.

As if the other three hundred sixty-four days of retail sales was not humbling enough, I was graced with learning the true heinous nature of the consumer on Black Friday. Male grizzly bears attacking the cubs of a female grizzly bear show more mercy than a human being in search of twenty percent off a mouse pad. Lines resembling Soviet breadlines from the 1970's began forming the night before this infamous day. Fist fights were not uncommon as the more ingenious of customers sought to contort and overlap the lines to their advantage. They often created serpentine like paths which would make even the award winning marching band choreographers jealous. These lines would then erupt into chaos as the doors flung open at six in the morning. Shopping carts became bumper cars, and stealing from another person's cart became acceptable. Parents would order their sleep-deprived children to guard the items in the cart while they dove into what resembled a rugby match scrum to get the latest video game. On Black Friday, we were no longer salespeople—we were traffic cops. We were the kind of traffic cops routinely shown on YouTube dancing like their pants are on fire as they try to control the million scooters, cars, bicycles, and trucks converging on the main traffic circle in a third-world country.

One of the toughest requirements about being a salesperson at Fry's Electronics was having a weekly sales quota to sell the company's extended warranties. These performance guaranties were extremely profitable for the company; therefore, the commissions on these were out of this world to motivate salespeople to sell it. The astronomical pressure of selling the extended warranties led to using tricky sales tactics to coerce customers to purchase them. The sneaky salespeople were like conniving snakes, waiting for innocent victims to make their kill. It was disgraceful and discomforting to witness a fellow salesperson use devious maneuvers on unassuming customers. If a Fry's Electronics salesperson did not meet your quota, they would be dismissed. The pressure of making the sales quota at the end of the week is like having the basketball with two seconds left while your team is losing the game by one point. Since being a survivor of the retail industry, I sympathize with those poor souls that have to suffer on their feet, submit to irrational customers, and be burdened with sales quotas. My hope for them is to find a way out of their retail Purgatory. I would never argue that working at Fry's Electronics is worse than delivering pizzas or cleaning bathrooms; but for me, it remains to be my absolute worst job experience. It left me with disgust for mean consumers, emotional paralysis on Black Fridays, and avoidance for commissioned salespeople. To this day, it gives me chills to think about working at Fry's Electronics, and not just because of my neuroma.

Will You Please Pass the Salt?

Joseph Coates
ENGL 1101

♦♦♦

When people think of sodium, they think of a seasoning that enhances the flavor of their food. Many Americans do not realize the health risks associated with this mineral, and if they do they either choose to regulate how much they consume or they choose to ignore it. The majority of Americans consume too much sodium. This quantity is very easy to exceed considering the amount of sodium used to manufacture processed foods. As of today, the mineral we know as sodium is considered safe for human consumption. However, many people dispute this theory. Currently the Food and Drug Administration (FDA) is being urged to regulate the sodium content in processed foods. As of right now there seems to be no limit to the amount of sodium food manufacturers can put in their products. A report commissioned by Congress "recommended that the FDA use its regulatory powers to declare that sodium above a certain level is unsafe" (Neuman 1). This regulation, however, may take some time to reach full effect because many consumers are accustomed to highly salted foods. The FDA should order "gradual reductions over time, to eventually reach healthier levels once taste and preferences have adjusted" (Neuman 1). The most important aspect is that Americans need to eat healthier, and the more options for healthier foods, the better.

The health risks associated with consuming high amounts of sodium are some of the most common seen today and can be severe in some cases. One of the major health risks linked to sodium is high blood pressure. "Scientists have known for decades that high sodium diets tend to raise blood pressure" (Jacobson 1). This has been an argument for some time and the time to address this issue is now. If the FDA had started regulating sodium content twenty years ago and slowly decreased the amount of sodium in processed foods, high blood pressure may not be such a huge issue today. There are a number of reasons why sodium elevates blood pressure. High blood pressure is not the only health risk from consuming sodium. It may also cause bone loss in older women. "In a two year study of postmenopausal women, researchers found that the higher a woman's sodium intake, the greater her bone loss at the hip" (Kuzemchak 1). These effects may be even worse for people who are thought to be sodium sensitive, such as African Americans and generally anybody over the age of fifty. Sodium sensitivity also increases with age and may be due to the same reasons why African Americans are sodium sensitive. Understanding the health risks associated with high sodium intake is important, and knowing whether or not an individual is sodium sensitive may benefit him or her greatly.

High blood pressure is just the beginning of what can result if an individual continues to consume high levels of sodium. There may be some people who are an exception to this, people who live their whole life with high blood pressure and never have a heart attack or a stroke. On top of that there may be some people who eat highly salted foods and never develop hypertension or high blood pressure. These people are lucky. Why take the risk of having a cardiac arrest, when it may be as simple as lowering your sodium intake as much as possible?

Sodium is not easy to avoid. Sodium is lurking in most processed foods available to Americans. The reasons for the excess amount of sodium in foods are not nearly as important as the reasons to eliminate it, or at least reduce it by half. When looking at the numbers they can be quite astonishing. "Some restaurant entrees have 2,000 milligrams or more in one dish, and fast food burgers can have more than 1,000 milligrams" (Hellmich 2). How are Americans supposed to lower their sodium intake, when one meal of the day contains the maximum recommended daily intake? These extremely high numbers involving sodium content are unfair to Americans and should not be tolerated. Many families in America cannot afford healthier meals and have no choice but to consume high sodium processed foods.

For consumers that are interested in lowering their sodium intake, there are steps to begin the process. Choose fresh foods that are not processed or prepared in restaurants. Some examples of these foods are fresh fruits and vegetables, all natural chicken or beef, and raw seeds and nuts. Next, if the only choice a consumer has is processed foods, choose the foods with the least sodium content. Lastly and perhaps the most important, is to be able to distinguish between low sodium and reduced sodium. These two terms have different meaning, and low sodium is the better of the two. Many people may believe that because the product says reduced sodium, they can consume more of the product and be fine, when in reality they may ultimately consume more than before.

There are many manufacturers of processed food products that are taking steps to lower the sodium content of their brands. These manufacturers may be taking these steps because they feel their cover has been blown and consumers are catching on to the effects of high sodium intake. The brands that are on this list include, but may not be limited to Campbell's, Frito-Lay, Orville Redenbacher, and Beech Nut. This is especially important for people who like to enjoy soups that are convenient and easy to make. Pepperidge Farm, which is the bread sector of Campbell's, "is rolling out lower sodium versions of the eight breads in its 100 percent natural line. Most will be down thirty-three to forty percent" says Tim Hasset (qtd. in Horovitz 1). Another manufacturer with normally high sodium content in their products is Orville Redenbacher. The next manufacturer to be mentioned and is possibly the most important sector of food products is a baby food manufacturer known as Beech Nut. This may be the most important sector of the food industry because the taste for highly salted food may begin at an early age. The last product to be reduced in sodium content is possibly the most interesting of the group. This product is sodium itself. All of these manufacturers are promoting a great cause and, in the future, hopefully more manufacturers will decide to contribute their part as well.

There is a factor that contributes to sodium content in foods, and this factor is one that cannot be controlled. Some prepared and processed foods require the use of salt for the production process. Cheese, for instance, needs sodium for the cheese curd process to occur. Many different types of bread also require the use of sodium in order for the rising process to occur. Another reason for the required use of sodium is that sodium is a natural preservative in many foods. This is an obstacle that may not be overcome, but as long as all other foods are lowered in sodium content, the ratio could very well balance out.

By reducing the amount of sodium in processed and prepared foods, many benefits may be accomplished. First of all, many lives could be saved. Lowering sodium content in foods lowers risk for developing high blood pressure that may lead to heart attacks or strokes. Reducing salt by just fifty percent in processed foods may lower the risk of other health issues as well. Until a regulation is put in place to control the amount of sodium in processed food products, consumers should be conscious of what they put into their bodies. People need to be mindful of the one life they have, and a life of high blood pressure, heart attacks, and strokes is not a life one should want to live.

Works Cited

Hellmich, Nanci. "Keeping A Lid on Salt: Not So Easy." *USA Today* 28 April 2010. Academic Search Complete. Web. 12 July 2010.

Horovitz, Bruce. "Some Brands Giving the Boot to Excess Salt." *USA Today* 25 Nov. 2008. Academic Search Complete. Web. 12 July 2010.

Jacobson, Michael. "Why the FDA Should Regulate Salt in Foods." *USNews* 25 May 2010. LexisNexis. Web. 14 July 2010.

Kuzemchak, Sally. "Stealth Salt." *Prevention* Mar. 2007: 59. Academic Search Complete. Web.12 July 2010.

Neuman, William. "F.D.A. is Urged to Set Limits for Levels of Salt in Foods." *The New York Times* 21 April 2010. Opposing Viewpoints Resource Center. Web. 14 July 2010.

"Shake Salt From Your Diet." *Consumer Reports* Jan. 2009. Print.

***

Why I Like This Essay: After serving in the U.S. Navy, Joseph Coates enrolled at GPC with the goal of transferring to a four-year college to complete a business degree. In this creative English 1101 essay, he argues that Americans need to cut back on their sodium intake in order to improve their health. Word choice is essential to good writing, and Joseph highlights the danger of sodium "lurking" in processed foods. Aware that affordability is a key factor, he also underscores that consumers and manufacturers must be responsible for finding solutions to the challenge of healthy eating.

While the topic itself is interesting, Joseph can also be commended for his writing strategies. Willing to tackle multiple drafts of the essay, he demonstrated the persistence needed for excellent academic work. Not only is the essay informative, but the writer's own lifestyle also supports the argument. Joseph has intentionally followed a low-sodium diet over a period of time, demonstrating that he is willing to take his own advice.

Jean Hakes, Instructor of English

Video Games' Influence
on Health and Behavior

Adrian Caldwell
ENGL 1101
♦♦♦

The philosopher Plato wrote that plays and poetry would corrupt and harm the youth. When the printing press made books available to the common man and novels flooded the market, they were accused of encouraging moral degeneracy. Today these forms of media are common, their consumption encouraged. Shakespeare, whose plays were vulgar in his own time, is now culturally pervasive. One of the most recent media to become popular, the video game, is now facing scrutiny similar to that of its ancestors. However, just as with the media that came before, these accusations are without merit. The potential for video games to inspire violence, potential cause addiction, or induce seizures is much less than its use as a positive tool for learning, socialization, treating Post-Traumatic Stress Disorder, and technological integration.

Opponents accuse video games of dehumanizing people, which in turn makes violence more culturally acceptable. According to studies analyzed by Dr. Art Markman, a psychology professor who specializes in behavior and motivation, players of violent video games, compared to neutral games such as Tetris, were more likely to display aggression towards others ("Video games, Violence, and Dehumanization"). When surveyed, they rated people dissimilar to themselves, such as immigrants, as having fewer qualities associated with humans. Given the opportunity, participants were also more likely to actively sabotage people's chances of employment based on perceived political differences. Dr. Markman believes that this demonstrates that violence within video games leads to players dehumanizing others with whom they have a lesser base of empathy, which itself leads to a higher incidence of players believing that violence towards people of dissimilar backgrounds is acceptable behavior.

While the studies mentioned do provide convincing evidence that players dehumanize others directly following playing violent video games, the evidence suggests only a short-term effect as a result of actual gameplay rather than existing personality flaws. Elizabeth Donovan, a therapist specializing in teenagers with behavioral problems, points out other studies that suggest actual violence in response to video games is perpetrated by people who have existing aggressive tendencies ("Video Game Violence: Does Player's Personality Matter More Than the Game?"). Even among these players, violent content in the games is less of a predictor of violence in real life than the level of competition within these games. A video game player throwing a tantrum is comparable to a board game player flipping the board; the fault does not lie with the game so much as the destructive player.

Another criticism of video games is that they have the capacity to be addictive, which is a major concern for parents and medical professionals alike. The American Academy of Pediatrics warns that excessive gaming can lead to increases in impulsiveness, depression, social phobia, and poor school performance ("Video Gaming Can Lead to Mental Health Problems"). The American Medical Association believes that 15% of children who play video games are addicted ("Is video-game addiction a mental disorder?"). There are support groups and treatment programs, and the Internet is rife with stories and confessions of video game addicts.

Although there is a strong indication that excessive consumption and problems with mood and socialization are related, researchers have failed to prove that video games are the causal agent. The Diagnostic and Statistical Manual, the authority on diagnoses of mental health, has rejected video game addiction for inclusion because there is a lack of research to indicate that such a thing exists. Anecdotal evidence cannot be taken into account because there are as many stories to indicate that depression and poor socialization leads to video game overuse as there are to indicate that overuse is a cause.

Because of the format of gameplay and comparable level of consumption among some players, many experts also compare so-called video game addiction to gambling addiction. One study found that extensive gameplay was attributed to increases in the production of dopamine, the brain chemical associated with addiction ("Teenage Video Game Players"). Pleasure centers of the brain were also shown to be larger in brain scans of individuals who played video games excessively rather than moderately.

However, comparisons between video games and gambling are inherently flawed. Peter Gray, a research professor of psychology whose specialty is developmental and educational psychology, explains why brain research is a flawed means of assessing addiction: "pleasure pathways" that light in brain scans when a person experiences addiction are indistinguishable from other types of pleasure ("Video Game Addiction: Does It Occur? If So, Why?"). Gray further criticizes the comparison, saying that gambling is entirely compulsive and irrational, and gamblers borrow, steal, and run themselves into ruin to feel the chemical rush of a win, whereas video gamers do not. Gambling games, by design, give an equal chance of success with every play and occasionally give players tangible rewards. Success in video games is dependent upon skill and effort, and the reward is only accomplishment.

Of the criticisms leveled against video games, their ability to induce seizures is the most concerning. Although most people who experience video game-induced seizures are epileptic or photosensitive, the experience can also be had by people who are hungry, thirsty, sleep-deprived, and otherwise stressed ("Video Game-Induced Seizures"). Most sufferers are children, making the possibility of a seizure especially concerning for children and their parents.

However, video game-induced seizures are easily preventable and only affect a small segment of the general population. Even among photosensitive individuals, video game-induced seizures are extremely rare ("Avoiding 'Pokemon' Seizures From TV, Video Games"). Guidelines for preventing these seizures are easy to follow and include such suggestions as sitting away from the television, playing in a well-lit room, reducing screen brightness, avoiding gameplay while tired, and taking breaks. The likelihood of seizures induced by exposure to television or video games also decreases with age.

One of the more positive aspects of video games is that they can encourage and supplement learning and mental development in children. Gray points out that because video game playing is usually a self-directed activity, the knowledge and skills children learn from video games is absorbed more effectively than learning which is forced onto them, and that children only engage in activities for several hours at a time if they benefit from the experience ("The Many Benefits, for Kids, of Playing Video Games"). Many video games have been demonstrated to improve problem solving abilities, working memory, critical thinking, and visual-spatial ability. Children who demonstrate lack of interest in reading and writing have the opportunity to improve their literacy through text-based communication within video games.

Video games also encourage social interaction. There is a class of games known as Massively Multiplayer Online Games through which thousands of players might interact competitively or socially. Other video games are designed to be played by multiple people in the same room and usually have a motion component, such as dancing or bowling. Even with games which are not designed to be played socially, players will swap tips, tricks, cheats, and custom content for improved gameplay. Video game culture has spawned several memes, forums, and even clubs through which players can make friends who share mutual interest.

Additionally, video games can be used to treat Post-Traumatic Stress Disorder. Bret A. Moore, a psychologist and veteran whose professional focus is the psychological health of service members, explains the process: traditionally, Post-Traumatic Stress Disorder is treated through exposure therapy using the patient's imagination to relive traumatic events and process them with the aid of a therapist, but virtual reality technology can supplement this treatment ("Video Games or Treatment for PTSD?"). With virtual reality, which is heavily derived from video game technology, the traumatic experience that the patient relives becomes less traumatic with repeated exposure. The United States military is already treating affected troops with virtual reality-supplemented therapy. As the technology develops, it could become available to civilians with

Post-Traumatic Stress Disorder such as victims of street violence or children from abusive homes.

Furthermore, video games prepare children for the workforce by teaching them how to interact with technology. There are very few jobs today which do not incorporate some type of electronic machine in an essential capacity. At the current rate that technology develops, it can only be expected that the use of technology to supplement or replace human work will increase. Video games themselves have even been shown to increase job performance in certain fields. The United States military uses video game simulations to train soldiers, and engaging, realistic gameplay has made soldiers more familiar with their weapons than soldiers in previous generations who did not have access to video game technology ("Virtual Reality Prepares Soldiers for Real War"). The Office of Naval Research even commissioned an online game called Massive Multiplayer Online Wargame Leveraging the Internet, or MMOWGLI, that they made available to the public in order to crowdsource strategies for combatting Somali Pirates ("Massive Multiplayer Online Wargame Leveraging the Internet"). Surgeons who regularly play video games display more speed and accuracy in their job performance than surgeons who do not play ("Research shows video games lead to fewer mistakes on the operating table").Video games provide an opportunity for children to learn and interact with technology so that they are more coordinated and technologically literate as adults. By denying children access to video games, parents would effectively deny them an important learning experience.

The positive effects of video games on players have been demonstrated to outweigh and outlast their negative effects. Violence and addiction as a result of gameplay is negligible. Video game-induced seizures, while a problem for some individuals, are rare even among people who are photosensitive. The educational, medical, and cultural potential for this medium is without limit. Over time, as video games' influence grows, the concerns for its potential for harm will dwindle. It is important to remember that all forms of expressive media have their merit, but they will only develop into beautiful and sophisticated art if they are allowed to flourish.

Works Cited

Cohen, Tamara. "Teenage Video Game Players Have Brains Like Gambling Addicts." *The Daily Mail*. Associated Newspapers Ltd. 11/15/2011. Web. 4/13/2012. <dailymail.co.uk>

Donovan, Elizabeth. "Video Game Violence: Does Player's Personality Matter More Than The Game?" *Psychology Today*. Sussex Publishers, LLC., 9/22/2011. Web. 2/18/2011. <psychologytoday.com>

Gray, Peter. "The Many Benefits for Kids, of Playing Video Games." *Psychology Today*. Sussex Publishers, LLC., 1/7/2012. Web. 2/18.2012. <psychologytoday.com>

- - -. "Video Game Addiction: Does It Occur? If So, Why?" *Psychology Today*. Sussex Publishers, LLC., 2/2/2012. Web. 2/18/2012. <psychologytoday.com>

Hitti, Miranda. "Avoiding 'Pokemon' Seizures From TV, Video Games." *WebMD Health News*. WebMD, LLC., 11/20/2005. Web. 4/19/2012. <webmd.com>

Markman, Art. "Video Games, Violence, and Dehumanization." *Psychology Today*. Sussex Publishers, LLC., 5/20/2011. Web. 2/18/2012. <psychologytoday.com>

"Massive Multiplayer Online Wargame Leveraging the Internet." *Office of Naval Research*. Web. 4/27/2012. <onr.navy.mil>

Moore, Bret A. "Video Games or Treatment for PTSD?" *Psychology Today*. Sussex Publishers, LLC., 5/24/2010. Web. 4/19/2012. <psychologytoday.com>

"Research Shows Video Games Lead to Fewer Mistakes on the Operating Table," *USA Today*. Gannet Co. Inc. 4/7/2004. Web. 4/27/2012. <usatoday.com>

Tanner, Lindsey. "Is Video-Game Addiction a Mental Disorder?" *Associated Press*. 6/22/2007. Web. 2/27/2012. <msnbc.msn.com>

Vargas, Jose Antonio. "Virtual Reality Prepares Soldiers for Real War." *The Washington Post*. 2/14/2006. Web. 4/27/2012. <washingtonpost.com>

"Video Gaming Can Lead to Mental Health Problems."
American Academy of Pediatrics. 1/17/2011. Web.
2/27/2012. <healthychildren.org>

***

Why I Like This Essay: From her first in-class writing sample
to her very polished final essay, "Video Games Influence on
Health and Behavior," Caldwell diligently completed each
writing assignment for English 1101. She is one of my finest
students to date, and this argumentative research paper justifies
why. Every time I teach the argumentative essay, I stress to my
students the importance of anticipating and addressing
counterpoints before presenting their own positions on a
controversial topic. This essay does just that, giving fair and
intelligent attention to the counterpoints. After addressing the
counterpoints, Caldwell convincingly presents her main points,
supporting each one with relevant and thorough research. It is
her explanation of the research that makes her essay standout to
me. Many students simply insert research without an explanation
as to how it ties back to the point being made. Caldwell,
however, synthesizes her research in a way that illustrates a
personal understanding of the information. This essay shows that
she owns her ideas and can think critically about ideas from
others. Moreover, the paragraphs flow effortlessly, a reflection
of the effort that went into arranging the points logically.
Caldwell has spared no creativity with her comprehensive use of
rhetorical devices, making this essay both informative and
interesting to read.
Alicia Guarracino, Instructor of English

When All God's Children Get Together

Vincent Roberts
ENGL 1101
♦♦♦

My search is born out of pain. It is born out of
confusion. Many tears have been shed prior to its labored
arrival. The conception was long before any announcement of
an I-search paper and the gestation period some thirty-five years.
Oh yes, it has truly been a paper conceived, birthed and labored
in love, and a need for acceptance. It is a paper that may be read
somewhat revolutionary and even controversial. However, the
need for the paper, in my opinion, far outweighs anything that
critics and the naysayers could ever argue.

Is there a place for a homosexual in heaven? I can hear
someone saying, "No, but there is a place for y'all in hell!" I beg
to differ. I am a child of God, and I am a homosexual. I know
on that great day when Gabriel's trumpet sounds and the dead in
Christ shall rise, I will meet my Maker and He will say, "Well
done son. Welcome Home!"

I hope to open someone's eyes. I hope to dispel the
untruth about homosexuality as an abomination and
condemnation to hell. I hope to free another child of God who is
homosexual from the chains that have bound me far too long.
And as God, The Great Orchestrator himself would have it, so
began my loosening experience.

I had just come home from a wonderful day at church,
will go unnamed to protect it from any haters. I couldn't wait to
share the marvelous, spirit-filled day of worship I had
experienced at this "gay church." Later on, after joining the
church, I was told by one of the ministers, "This isn't a gay
church, but the Lord's church." However, it was categorized; I
couldn't wait to tell someone about how the powerful presence
of God couldn't be contained by the doors of the sanctuary and
rushed out as a mighty tidal wave drowning everyone in its path.
Before I could make it into the sanctuary, I found myself
standing in the vestibule speaking in tongues, trying to hold my

peace as not to "tear up" the vestibule with a praise dance. I wanted to share how beautifully the anointed choir sang that morning. I wanted to share how the pastor, also homosexual, could teach as well as preach the Word. I wanted everyone to know how all these stud lesbians, decked out in two-piece suits, flaming homosexuals in drag, even your everyday conservative homosexual brother, "misfits" other churches talk about and throw away, were going for it in the name of Jesus.

I wanted someone to know that the same power of God I had seen move "straight churches" for the past six years, also moved at a "gay church." I chose to share my experience with one of my Christian brothers from the "straight church" that I had attended over the past six years. He was the same man who sat at my hospital bed when I was sick. He was the man I'd come to love as the brother I never had. He was a man of God whom I was sure could appreciate the mighty move of God I had just witnessed. To my utter surprise, his response was not one of admiration, but one of prejudice. "That doesn't sound like a church I'd ever want to go to, brother; it sounds like Sodom and Gomorrah to me," said my little brother in Christ. His words stung my already fragile spirit as though I had been slapped in the face. I couldn't believe he had just said that to me. I didn't know how to respond. I hung up the phone so stunned I couldn't even cry. The tears would not come until the next morning, and when they did come, years of pain and anguish came with them.

In the meantime, as I washed my dishes and prepared my Sunday dinner, I heard God's voice in my spirit. He said, "There was a day in time when the white man believed that the black man was a second class, sub-human species, and the majority believed it was right, so they wrote it down in their books. There was a day in time when the white man said that women were a second class, sub-human species, and again the majority believed it was right. Therefore, it too was written in the law books. There was a day in time when man believed that homosexuals were a second class, sub-human species, and it was written as law. A homosexual can't change his or her sexual orientation any more than a black man can make his skin white or a woman become a man." I had never heard anything so profound about homosexuality before that made as much sense.

Chains broke off me that very day. My spiritual walk with Christ was forever changed. I would never go back to the bondage of religion that I had previously known.

Although freed from the chains that had bound me for years, my mentality was still that of a person imprisoned. The chains had been broken, but now there was the matter of walking in my new freedom. Throughout my life, the general sentiment I had heard about homosexuality was that "it is wrong." I spent the past thirty-five years trying to be more boyish and straight acting. These thoughts played through my mind like a broken record. I wasn't tough enough. I was too effeminate. Little boys don't cry. Boys are supposed to play sports. I didn't excel in sports. I tried to be the boy whom society, my parents included, said I had to be. I dated girls, but in the back of my mind, I wondered what it would be like to be with a boy. I tried to change. I had prayed and cried, and cried and prayed. I spent many years hating that side of me that wasn't like the other boys. I wasn't comfortable in my skin; consequently, I was equally uncomfortable in society. I just didn't fit in. Now to find a church where there were others like me, and to be told I was still "wrong," was yet another blow to my already low self-esteem. Even though I thought I was liberated through the mighty power of God, I still suffered from years of shame and psychological abuse. My spirit was wounded.

That shame recently reared its ugly head again while I was in the library researching material for my college English class. When I placed the words "is there a place for a homosexual in heaven," in the Galileo search engine, I didn't get a response. I then asked Amelia, the librarian, for help.

"Well," she said in an audible voice enough for people ten feet away to hear, "try putting in homosexuality and religion."

Feeling ashamed, I could have crawled under the desk. Damn, did she have it to say it out loud? I felt the same shame while sitting with another librarian trying to get resources for my paper. She too had no problem talking out loud about my topic. I was the one with the problem. I had even gone as far as expressing to my professor that I didn't want to bring my rough draft to our class workshop because I didn't want to share my essay with my classmates. I didn't want to have to defend myself. I am tired of fighting. I have struggled and fought with this all my life, and I am just tired of fighting.

To my surprise, my search revealed vast amounts of information. My paper isn't so revolutionary after all. Even the words spoken in my spirit about homosexuality weren't necessarily new ideas. I came across a book titled Their Own Receive Them Not by Horace L. Griffin. The first chapter of the book echoes the words I had heard in my spirit about homosexuality, gender, and race. Griffins said that hatred towards blacks and homosexuals are indeed parallel and are a part of our great nation's past. The black church was always there to support the cause of racism, but when it came time to lending support to fight that same hatred expressed towards another group of human beings, specifically homosexuals, they were nowhere to be found. In fact, in many cases, the black churches were vehement supporters of prejudice against homosexuals. This was so ironic because they too had been victims of the same type of prejudice and discrimination (9-10).

I recently learned that I can't argue about my being a homosexual and a man of God. Most people are going to reject the idea right off the bat. Our thoughts and ideas are formed, for the most part, by what we learn in our households, and our local, as well as national communities. Generally speaking, Western ideas about men, women, families, and how we interact with one another, are shaped by the Bible. We take our cues about what is right or wrong from the Bible, and heaven forbid you are operating out of the principles expressed in it. You're either a hypocrite, a sinner, a lukewarm Christian, or even worse as in the case of a homosexual, an abomination. The age old joke is God made Adam and Eve not Adam and Steve. Often times, these ideas, these beliefs, misinterpretations and misinformation about the Bible have been passed on from one generation to the next while at the same time passing on ignorance and hate, disguising them as the truth.

Probably, the most misinterpreted text in the Bible, in regards to homosexuality, is the story of Sodom and Gomorrah. Many people use this scripture to argue that homosexuality is wrong, an abomination, and to assassinate homosexuals. The story makes reference to the men of Sodom wanting "to know" Lot's guests (Holy Bible King James Version Gen. 19: 1-11). Many opponents of homosexuality interpret this text as the men of Sodom wanting to have sex with Lot's guests and the reason for the destruction of the city. Daniel A. Helminiak points out the real reason for the destruction of Sodom and Gomorrah in his book What the Bible Really Says about Homosexuality:

> The whole story and its culture make clear that
> the author was not concerned about sex in itself,
> and it was irrelevant whether the sex was hetero-
> or homosexual. In place of his male guest, without
> a second thought Lot offered his daughters. The
> point of the story is not sexual ethics. The story of
> Sodom is no more about sex than it is about pounding
> on someone's front door. In the story of Sodom, both
> the sex and the pounding are incidental to the main
> point of the story. The point is abuse and assault,
> in whatever form they take. To use this text to condemn
> homosexuality is to misuse this text. (47)

He further contends that the Bible itself makes clear the sin of Sodom was not about homosexuality as "state[d]...baldly to the prophet Ezekiel. This was the guilt of your sister Sodom: she and her daughters had pride, surfeit of food and prosperous ease, but did not aid the poor and needy. The sin of Sodomites was that they refused to take in the needy travelers" (48).

As many scriptures that seemingly point to the "sin" of homosexuality, there are just that many that point out the love and compassion of Christ. So let's presuppose homosexuality is a sin for those in favor of condemning the homosexual. In a conversation with Reverend Dr. Sheila Manner, a minister of the Gospel for forty years and my spiritual mother, I asked, "Pastor, I love God more than many heterosexual people I know; why am I condemned?" She referred me to a scripture in the Bible in the book of Luke where Jesus was invited to a feast at the home of a Pharisee. Pharisees were known to be religious leaders who followed the religious laws perfectly. A woman who was a sinner showed up at the feast uninvited and fell at the feet of Jesus. In essence, through her washing, kissing and anointing his feet, she worshipped him. The Pharisee was appalled. Jesus blasted the Pharisee and told him, you know the law, but haven't done half as much as this sinner. He told the woman her sins were forgiven, and her faith had saved her (Holy Bible King James Version Luke 7:36-50). My spiritual mother said, "You're that woman."

John J. McNeil, a Catholic priest and psychotherapist, wrote in The Church and the Homosexual:

> Homosexuals within the Church have...a right to seek ways to resolve...injustice. [T]he Church can attain true consciousness of the injustices which the homosexual suffers and a real process can begin of separating the wheat from the chaff, the true implications of Christian faith and morality for the homosexual from the misunderstandings and prejudices...(195)

Many Christians believe that we make up the body of Christ. If we concede to this notion, Christ is certainly broken into pieces. Instead of loving one another, as we are all children of God, we waste precious time tearing each other down, leaving the body of Christ divided. I've heard it said, united we stand and divided we fall. How can the love of Christ be effectively spread when there is hate and division in the church? I believe some people are going to be surprised on that day when all God's children get together that His homosexual children with be there too.

Works Cited

Griffin, Horace L. Their Own Receive Them Not. Cleveland.
    The Pilgrim Press, 2006. 9-10. Print.
Helminiak, Daniel A., Ph.D., and John S. Spong. What the Bible
    Really Says About Homosexuality. Millennium Edition.
    Tajique: Alamo Square Press, 2000. 47-48. Print.
Manner, Sheila Reverend Dr. Personal Interview. July 2010
McNeill, John J. The Church and the Homosexual. 4th ed.
    Boston. Beacon Press, 1993. 195. Print.
The Holy Bible. Ed. Russell L. Surls. Grand Rapids. World
    Publishing, 1996. Print. Authorized King James Vers.

***

Why I Like This Essay: "When All God's Children Get Together" fully meets and surpasses the requirements of the original essay assignment: an "I-search" essay that details a research journey. This essay's crowning achievement is its relentless, dogged pursuit of a possibly unanswerable question. It challenges authority, and it's not afraid to convey dismay and even anger. It doesn't follow the strictures of a conventional essay, nor does it have to—but at the end we see the writer making great strides toward resolving this tough question.
Michael Diebert, Associate Professor of English

Does Prevention Kill?

Stephanie Moore
ENGL 1101
♦♦♦

In his book *Vaccine: The Controversial Story of Medicine's Greatest LifeSaver,* Arthur Allen relates a disturbing story. In 2004, a Colorado infant named Evelina Moran became sick with pertussis, commonly known as whooping cough. Curled into a ball, her face turning blue, the child ended up in neonatal intensive care. Five weeks later, she would come home with scarred lungs and over $200,000 in medical expenses. Her mother most likely brought the illness home from an unvaccinated patient at the dental office where she worked (353). Because children like baby Evelina become collateral damage, the choice not to vaccinate one's child is controversial. Those who make that choice maintain that there is a mountain of evidence to prove that vaccines are ineffective, cause debilitating illness and are part of a malicious medical establishment motivated by greed. Despite their claims that the risks outweigh the benefits, the evidence shows that vaccination is a relatively safe, effective way to combat disease.

History is the best evidence for the value of vaccination. According to *The Vaccine Controversy: The History, Use and Safety of Vaccines* by Kurt Link, prior to the introduction of the rubella vaccine in 1965, the nation witnessed "2,100 deaths at birth, 6,250 miscarriages; 8,055 deaf children; 3,580 deaf-blind children; 1,790 mentally retarded children; 6,575 abnormalities; 5,000 therapeutic abortions,' due to congenital rubella syndrome. As of 2005, there were no reported cases of congenital rubella syndrome in the United States (84). While the evidence for vaccines eliminating diseases is abundant, we also see people giving up their vaccines and experiencing negative results. In postwar Japan, 150 per 100,000 people contracted whooping cough. Vaccination brought the number down to 0.2 per 100,000 in 1950. However, according to Link, after the unfortunate deaths of two children from complications related to the whole cell vaccine in 1975, vaccination rates began to drop. By 1979, Japan was again experiencing an epidemic (67-68).

Other studies have also recorded the effects of non-vaccination. Elizabeth Fair, in a 2002 article published by the American Academy of Pediatrics entitled "Philosophic Objection to Vaccination as a risk for Tetanus Among Children Younger than 15 years," notes that only fifteen cases of childhood tetanus occurred between 1992 and 2000. Of those children, twelve had never been vaccinated because of religious objection (most were Amish). The three who were previously vaccinated had milder symptoms and shorter hospital stays that the children who had never been vaccinated (Fair).

Anti-vaccination activists also claim that chronic childhood disabilities are caused by vaccination. In 1998, a British doctor named Andrew Wakefield and several co-authors published a paper claiming to have found a link between the MMR vaccine and autism. The Canadian Paediatric Society (CPS), in a 2007 paper entitled "Autism Spectral Disorder: No Causal Relationship with Vaccines" points out the flaws in Wakefield's study. The results were based on only eight children, whose parents claimed their symptoms began days after the MMR shot (CPS). Anti-vaccine protestors claimed that thimerosal, which contains an organic form of mercury, is the cause of these symptoms (CPS), even though other studies could not replicate Wakefield's results. Vaccines containing thimerosal were removed from the market in 2000 as a precaution. Since then, the rates of autism in children have remained the same. In Canada, however, thimerosal was removed from routine vaccines in 1996. Canada still has rising autism rates.

The anti-vaccination movement is based on distrust and misguided nostalgia. Mainstream medicine, vaccine opponents claim, is controlled by money-hungry pharmaceutical companies. The implication is that people who work in "natural medicine" do not also request money for services. The alternative healing business is lucrative and would be more so if they could prove their techniques actually work. Why would pharmaceutical companies embrace vaccination if they could make money with less painful treatments that worked? Modern medicine is based on science: experiment, trial and error, and research. The anti-vaccination movement is based on emotional appeals and post hoc reasoning.

Many people claim that not vaccinating is a personal choice. While it is a right, it is not entirely personal. People who forgo vaccines can count on the vaccinated people around them not to spread disease. This is called herd immunity (353). The more unvaccinated people there are, the less herd immunity we have. When the unvaccinated fall ill, the cost of caring for them far exceeds the cost of inoculation. Non-vaccination places a greater burden on an already burdened health care system. It puts other people at risk. If more people understood the reality of the diseases we vaccinate against, this movement would not be so powerful.

Works Cited

Allen, Arthur. Vaccine: *The Controversial Story of Medicine's Greatest Lifesaver*. New York: Norton, 2007. Print.

Canadian Paediatric Society. "Autism Spectrum Disorder: No Causal Relationship with Vaccines." *Paediatrics and Child Health* 12.5 (2007). 393-395. Web. March 30, 2011.

Fair, Elizabeth. "Philosophical Objection to Vaccination as a Rick for Tetanus Among Children Younger than 15 Years." *Pediatrics: Official Journal of the American Academy of Pedatrics*.109.1.e2 (2002) Web. March 29, 2011.

Link, Kurt. *The Vaccine Controversy: The History, Use and Safety of Vaccinations*. Westport: Praeger, 2005. Print.

***

Why I Like This Essay: Right at the first, Stephanie grabs us with a paradoxical title that makes us want to read further because we wonder what on earth could prevent something and kill at the same time. Her introduction begins with a brief narrative example designed to engage our emotions on a topic of current concern: the safety of childhood vaccinations. After offering a clear thesis, she presents evidence, introducing sources in a way that reveals their credentials, thus building her own credibility. Opting for the classical or Aristotelian argument structure, Stephanie addresses the opposition last. Such a decision can be a disaster for less skilled writers because they might leave the audience agreeing with the opposition. Stephanie is up to the task, however, because she effectively counters the opposing points. Her conclusion directs readers to consider the impact on our health care system and society as a whole if we fail to vaccinate our children

Dr. Sandra Matthews, Professor of English

To Move or Not to Move:
That Is the Question

Katie Tamashevich
ENGL 1101H
◆◆◆

    Immigration is a political and social phenomenon that has been known to mankind for generations. It is the driving force of the world's economic and social development and a contributing factor of the ethnic structure of many societies. The dictionary defines immigration as movement of non-native people into a country in order to settle there. It is a dry definition behind which lie many destinies, family histories, stories of success, failure, realized dreams and hopes. And even though it may pose more advantages than disadvantages to those relocating, it nevertheless contains many hidden obstacles and hardships for the ex-patriots seeking a new home abroad. There are a great number of factors that determine the choice of a country for relocation. The general trend is to move from less developed countries to those better developed socially and economically. In history many migration trends have been determined by specific events, such as armed conflicts, persecution, at times genocide or ethnic cleansing of the native population in certain areas. Certain political regimes gaining power have resulted in several waves of migration to safer and more favorable parts of the world.

    The modern migration trends are very similar to those that have been established during the course of history. A large number of people from all parts of the world choose to find a new home outside of their native environment in which they were born due to several factors. These factors are commonly called the push and pull factors. In other words, they are reasons forcing native population to leave their homeland and advantages attracting them to seek residency elsewhere. Indeed, often a new country means new opportunities and a chance to improve the quality of life. The main push factors of immigration are poor economies, lack of employment, famine, warfare, oppression, persecution, restrictions on practicing religion or inability to seek education. Many developed countries offer a great number of possibilities to their citizens and therefore become appealing to new immigrants. The main pull factors, attracting new immigrants are mainly economical, political, religious and personal, such as re-uniting with family members or marriage. For some immigration is a way to live their dream, to others sometimes it is the only opportunity to break away from the chains of the society into which they are born. A great example would be expatriates from the Middle East moving to different parts of Europe and United States. Among other advantages, it has given many women an opportunity to seek education. However, no matter how appealing the new opportunities may seem, there are a number of drawbacks in relocation that one should consider prior to emigrating.

Along with many advantages that the new state of residency may offer, there are a great number of obstacles and new circumstances new immigrants have to deal with upon arrival. The biggest sacrifice many people have to make before departing from their homeland is leaving their families, friends, culture and habitual environment behind. And hardship does not stop at that. Upon arrival to their new country of residency many immigrants find it difficult to adjust in the new society. Finding a place to live, looking for a job, learning a new language, adjusting mentally and psychologically – these are just a few difficulties on their way to a happier future. Very often immigrants have to deal with discrimination and hostility towards them from the local population. It is a common practice for a certain percentage of foreigners unable to adjust and assimilate to return to their home countries.

As an immigrant in the first generation, I have lived through both happiness and sadness of choosing a new homeland. It has definitely given me better opportunities of education and employment and a freedom of speech and actions, something that I had experienced a lack of growing up in Belarus. However, the separation from the family and friends and my own culture and environment at times seems unbearable. I strongly believe that it is up to every individual whether or not to learn the new mentality and choose to adjust and accept a new culture. I personally have enjoyed this journey greatly, grateful for every opportunity hidden in my quest of living my American Dream.

Immigration has been proven many times to be the driving force of the world economy. Many countries welcome and encourage new residents, benefitting greatly from this useful policy. It often causes brain drain to the states that are left behind. Many of the great men and women who have made their names in history have immigrated from different parts of the world. To choose immigration or to stay patriotic towards their native country is a difficult decision to make. My greatest hope is that everyone who takes that uneasy step will find their happiness in the end of their journey.

***

Why I Like This Essay: Katie Tamashevich started college at the Minsk State Linguistic University in Belarus before immigrating to the US and coming to Georgia Perimeter College. This well-written essay demonstrates her talents with languages. It is also analytical, expanding on personal experience in ways most people can understand, and expressive, bringing out the bittersweet experience of moving to a foreign land. I am proud of the opportunities we offer our students at GPC and glad to have students like Katie.

Ted Wadley, Associate Professor of English

The Price to Dance

Olivia Hightower
ENGL 1101H
♦♦♦

Music filled the air as little pink balls of fluff swirled around me. With hearts beaming with joy, my little ballerina students pirouetted and leapt across the room in their pink frilly tutus. As I congratulated each one on a beautiful arabesque, I could not help but reflect on my first ballet class fifteen years ago. It was my lifelong dream to be a prima ballerina. My little ballet girls also dream of becoming ballerinas one day. Yet, as I watched them practice tondue and pas de chat happily in their tutus barely covering their portly waists, little did they know the price a ballerina must pay to dance. Although there are numerous styles of dance, ballet is the one that taught me the most discipline, dedication, and determination.

My first day in a ballet studio overwhelmed me. Teachers shouted at me different orders: "Hold your back up! Tighten your core! Turn your feet out! Do not bend your knees! Bend your knees! Point your toes!" Every muscle in my body screamed in protest at the seemingly impossible task it was asked to perform. The unnatural positions threatened to produce a week of discomfort and soreness. The one word that was repeated constantly was "discipline." Discipline the body to reach beyond its limits; discipline the mind to persevere; discipline the soul not to lose heart. Balance, coordination, and rhythm all play a key factor to dancing the steps well. One must achieve the step perfectly at precisely the correct count or risk ruining the combination. Discipline is making a complicated step look effortless by gliding gracefully about the stage.

Without dedication, a ballet dancer cannot develop discipline. Dance is not only an art and a sport, but also a lifestyle. One must have great dedication and be completely devoted to dance. When I did ballet full time, every spare moment was dedicated to dancing. I was in the studio six days a week, five to six hours a day. Family vacations, social events, and other opportunities were sacrificed for ballet. Other interests such as art, music, and acting were put away, for it was impossible to do other activities outside of ballet. Not only was there not time to do any other activities, but the strenuous physical weight dancing demands was enough to carry by itself. Most ballet dancers retire before they turn thirty because their bodies are so exhausted. To a dancer, this lifestyle is normal. The dedication of that level is expected or assumed. A dancer must be willing to give up all. Unexpected costumes, leotards, tights, hair supplies, and pointe shoes costs are all a part of the dedication. Most pointe shoes cost up to ninety dollars a pair. Depending on how fast a dancer breaks them in, pointe shoes last only for a few months.

In addition to discipline and dedication, a successful dancer needs determination. For instance, a tone-deaf dancer may struggle with the counts, steps, and combinations and is doomed to fail if not for determination. When I started dancing, I was not only tone-deaf, but also I was clumsy and awkward. I was half a beat slower most of the time and half a beat faster the rest of the time. I had to be trained to hear the beat and make the steps follow the beat. After the first class, I went home and cried. The criticism, rejection, and pain were enough to make me want to never set foot in another studio again. Yet, the next day I went back to ballet class because I was determined to succeed and to not give up. Dancing well took years of dedication and hours to learn complicated combinations. When I make blunder in a combination, I repeat the steps until I have it correctly. Although my fatigued body screams for a rest, my determination refuses to stop. One must be completely determined to perfect the steps and work extremely hard for very little recognition. In the world of dance, competition is high. Only the determined succeed.

Although I did not proceed in my endeavors with a professional ballet career, I was able to learn the lessons ballet taught me of discipline, dedication, and determination. I learned the art of discipline in learning the steps and training my body to stretch itself; I found the character of dedication in persevering and not giving up; and I discovered the pleasure of determination in working hard and succeeding. When I watch a ballet, I think about the hard work and hours a ballerina sacrificed to be there dancing on stage. The lifestyle of a dancer is a hard road to travel. It is filled with little pay, little sleep, and little recognition. Yet thousands of girls and boys pay the physical, financial, and emotion price to dance each year because the applause after a performance pays more than any salary. Perhaps someday my little ballerinas will come to learn the lessons of ballet; not only the lessons of plié and tondue that I teach them, but also learning the lessons of discipline, dedication, and determination. Perhaps they, too, someday will pay the price to dance.

***

Why I Like This Essay: Liv Hightower is a talented student, who in addition to dancing and writing well, appeared in a GPC production of Shakespeare's Midsummer Night's Dream. In this essay, she speaks from the heart about the joy of performance and the effort required for success.

Ted Wadley, Associate Professor of English

Licensed to Live

Aleksandr Wobeck
ENGL 1101H
♦♦♦

Sheer ecstasy ran through my veins as I pulled out of the driveway in my navy blue Ford Focus, by myself. I had been granted a gift ever so simple but still unbelievable: my license. The moment of my first drive was full of excitement as well as some fears. The initial euphoria of having complete control of my time was freeing, but the happiness was followed by disappointment after realizing I was alone, and then the drive finished with the knowledge that my license was a positive landmark in my life. For the first time ever, I was empowered with my own transportation.

The ability to finally control my direction was amazing. Prior to receiving their licenses, most teenagers complain about their parents having to drive them, but, my circumstance was an extreme. Ever since I could remember, both my parents had worked fulltime. Due to their work hours, my parents were not able to drive me places. Throughout seventh and eighth grade, I hid from security a couple of times because my mother could not manage to race over to Lovett before the school closed. Not having rides continued throughout my high school years at Riverwood. When I started at GPC, I had one class on Tuesday and Thursday from ten to eleven. However, I had to come at seven in the morning and leave at six in the evening. Needless to say, I cherished the end of my waiting. The control brought me joy, but it also alarmed me that I could no longer depend on my parents.

My independence made me aware of my disappearing parental "safety net." More often than not, I was responsible for life's daily tasks; I was expected to do my own laundry, keep my room tidy, and excel in academics without any reinforcement from my parents. However, one of the tasks that I always relied on my parents for was transportation. Through long hours in daily car rides, my mother and I had developed an incredibly strong relationship. I feared that our friendship would start to crumble without our "car time" together. My rush of unexpected emotions frightened me. I felt that I was naïve for not appreciating my parents. I knew that I had lost a part of myself forever. Fortunately, the panicked feeling of loneliness was dismissed as I thought about the new benefits of my license.

The card in my wallet had transformed into a ticket that would lead me to new adventures in my life. I was an avid horseman who had previously struggled to achieve my goals. Laguna Stables, my barn in Alpharetta, was thirty miles from my home in Sandy Springs. The distance was always challenging to cope with. I was formerly hindered from the inability to ride my horses whenever I pleased or to attend competitions when my mother was working. I was now able to train at the highest level possible. Today, I realize that my goals would have been unachievable had it not been for my license. I am now able to attend competitive circuits that last weeks. One example of this is HITS in Ocala, FL. These circuits are going to be cherished throughout my life. Overall, the 3.5 by 2" plastic brought strange feelings of ecstasy, terror, and hope in a mere one hour span.

I realize that my license will transform me into a new person without bounds. My license had prepared me become an individual in the world. I had experienced happiness, sorrow, and maturity due to my driving privileges. The freedom from my parents' grasp was exhilarating but, it also brought on feelings of regret. I now understand that my license will mold me into my future self. But now I cannot afford to wait and debate the issue, I have places I need to drive to!

***

Why I Like This Essay: Alek Wobeck has written a fine vignette, a coming-of-age experience almost universal in our society. Other students, faculty, every reader will be able to identify with being able to drive on one's own.
Ted Wadley, Associate Professor of English

The Demise of Print Journalism

Samuel Lack
ENGL 1101H
♦♦♦

News has always served an important role in people's lives. When the printing press was invented by Johannes Gutenberg during the 15th century, the way in which news would be delivered to people would be forever changed. Preceding this amazing invention, news and village stories had to be passed on via word of mouth or written on parchment. The printing press allowed people to create many copies of the news. Since Gutenberg's invention, print news has changed in many ways. Today, the print journalism industry includes local, national and international news. There is news about economics, sports, entertainment, food, health and many other interesting topics. Print journalism companies control what information is included in their material based on their readership. Print journalism companies include in their material what their readers are most interested in so that they can make money. However, in recent decades, print journalism companies have lost large sums of money. Journalism companies' major problem is that they are not creating enough revenue from advertising. Also, they must now deal with "an Internet culture built on free content" (Kurtz). Just like people made improvements to the printing press following its introduction, print journalism companies now need to make improvements to the way in which they deliver their news as well. In this technologically savvy era, print journalism companies are experiencing a decline in their profit. In order to keep making money, magazine and newspaper companies are digitally publishing their material.

Print journalism companies are now digitally publishing their material because they are losing customer loyalty. To some customers, newspapers and magazines are charging too much money. In society today there is competition in all industries, especially in the news industry. Customers are changing their subscriptions to other sources of news because they are able to pay a smaller fee or no fee at all for the same information. In some cases, newspaper customers had completely dropped their subscriptions because "newspapers had become too cautious, too incremental and too dull, tailored largely for insiders" (Kurtz). Companies are also losing customers because their delivery frequency can be a nuisance to buyers. Some magazines are only delivered once every two weeks or in some cases once every three months. Readers want to be able to receive information more frequently and they are switching to options that allow them to more readily access it. If print journalism companies don't switch to digital circulation then they will lose many of their customers.

Another reason print journalism companies are digitally publishing their material is in order to save money. Fewer jobs are needed if all information is made available digitally. Also, less money is spent on printing the news because the volume of print subscribers will decrease. As print companies digitally publish their material, the information will be immediately accessible. Before this change, the news took longer to get to the public because time was spent on printing the material and then sending it out. By reducing their fixed and variable costs through digital publishing, print journalism companies are able to increase their profit.

One way in which print journalism companies are making money by digitally publishing their material is through the Internet. First, companies must go digital by "building sites that draw users and traffic, then capitalizing on user data through permission marketing and behavioral targeting" ("Critical Thinking"). By posting their material on a website, companies can charge a smaller fee for their readers because there are fewer costs. There are several ways in which companies are charging for access to online content. In one case, newspaper or magazine companies may charge readers a monthly or annual fee for access to their website. An alternative method is to allow readers to access most of the content online for free but charge for complete access. For example, ESPN.com allows anyone to read articles on its website about the most popular sports stories. However, for up to date sports rumors and other breaking news consumers must pay a monthly or annual fee to be an "ESPN Insider."

Some magazine companies are giving their loyal print customers full access to their online content. In ESPN's case, those who subscribe to ESPN the Magazine are automatically ESPN Insiders and have complete online viewing privileges. In the case of MediaNews, "in order to prepare for a paperless future, the company has emphasized digital sales that are not bundled with print" (Carr). Another incentive for print journalism companies to put their material online is unlimited ad space. Journalism companies are now able to charge less money to companies wishing to advertise and they can have unlimited advertisers as well. Publishing content online allows journalism companies to maintain customer loyalty and save money, which leads to a larger profit.

Another way journalism companies have digitally published their material is through applications for smart-phones, tablet computers, and other electronic devices. Many news apps are free but have ads. Apps give users access to newspapers or magazines on the go and anytime or anywhere. Journalism companies are able to take advantage of some apps due to their unique features. For example, Twitter is an easy way for journalism companies to spread news to all of their followers in 140 characters or fewer. Many companies use *Twitter* because "it's a direct link to elusive and valuable audiences" (Palser). Some of these audiences might be "younger people who are interested in certain kinds of news but don't spend all their time on news Web sites" (Palser). Even though journalism companies can't charge readers to view their posts on third party apps, newspaper and magazine companies, such as *The New York Times* and *The Washington Post*, have created their own apps that charge customers for use. Journalism companies' efforts to release news via apps on smart-phones, tablet computers, and other electronic devices have helped them stay relevant with today's technology and create profit.

In our world today, technology plays a very large role in every aspect of our lives. In order to cope with the sudden popularity of electronics and the Internet, print journalism companies have begun to digitally publish their content. Print journalism companies have lost money in recent years because they are losing customers and costs have risen. In order to change their chances "newspapers with weak market penetration or ones that face intense competition may need to target a specific audience" ("Critical Thinking"). Journalism companies have made an effort to counter recent losses by publishing their material online and through apps in hopes of future profits. Even though print journalism companies are experiencing a major change in their industry, "what they do has an impact beyond their readers and advertisers" (Kurtz). These companies continue to publish high-quality content every day and will continue to do so even if they must make sacrifices in the short run. In the eyes of John Paton, CEO of *MediaNews*, "a third of the news will be expensive local content produced by professional journalists, a third will come from readers and community input, and a third will be aggregated" (Carr). Regardless of the way in which news is presented to readers, it will continue to have a significant impact on the way we live our lives every day.

Works Cited

Carr, David. "Newspapers' Digital Apostle." *Nytimes.com*. New York Times, 20 Nov. 2011. Web. 20 Nov. 2011.

"Critical Thinking." Editor & Publisher 144.3 (2011): 15.Academic Search Complete. Web. 20 Nov. 2011.

Kurtz, Howard. "The Death of Print?" *Washingtonpost.com*. Washington Post, 11 May 2009. Web. 20 Nov. 2011.

Palser, Barb. "Hitting the Tweet Spot." *American Journalism Review* 31.2 (2009): 54. Academic Search Complete. Web. 20 Nov. 2011

***

Why I Like This Essay: Sam Lack declared a radio/television major as a dual-enrollment student (that is, while still in high school). This research paper demonstrates his interest in journalism with good coverage of the prospects new technologies offer, as well as the dangers for printed media. His research is sound, and his own ideas are clear. Perhaps other young people will read his work and join him in building a brave, new future.

Ted Wadley, Associate Professor of English

Symbols of Joy and Sorrow in Chopin's *The Story of an Hour*

Drew Bannister
ENGL 1102

♦♦♦

In Kate Chopin's "The Story of an Hour," Mrs. Louise Mallard is a "woman afflicted with heart trouble." (287). She is gently informed by her loved ones that her husband, Brently Mallard, was killed in a recent train accident and begins to weep immediately upon hearing the tragic news. When her grief passes, she secludes herself in her bedroom where the majority of the story's theme is revealed, primarily through symbolism. Louise contemplates her current situation and eventually discovers that her grief is fleeting. She becomes overwhelmed by discovering an unfamiliar sense of joy in that she has a future that is no longer limited to simply being a wife. Louise now views herself as a free individual who is in control of her own fate. During the ironic climax, her husband Brently Mallard unexpectedly returns home. When Louise sees him, her "troubled heart" stops at the sight of him, causing her to die. In "The Story of an Hour" Chopin effectively uses symbolism to vividly illustrate the mixed feelings of joy and sorrow that Louise Mallard experiences.

The armchair that Louise takes refuge in after locking herself in her room is the first use of symbolism by Chopin to convey a sense of joy that Louis is beginning to feel. "There stood, facing the open window, a comfortable roomy armchair. Into this she sank, . . ." (288). The armchair is described as "comfortable" and "roomy" leading the reader to understand that Louise is comforted by the idea of personal space. This is confirmed later when Chopin writes, "There would be no one to live for during those coming years; she would live for herself." (288). The open window that the chair faces is an essential use of symbolism that Chopin utilizes to aid in Louise's character development. The "comfortable armchair facing an open window" illustrates Louise looking from her current situation toward the future. Louise's reaction to the setting outside of the window expresses that she is starting to gain a positive outlook on her situation, and is obtaining a sense of modest relief which later develops into a private elation.

The view from Louise's window depicts a pleasant spring day and symbolizes a new beginning. "She could see in the open square before her house the tops of trees that were all aquiver with the new spring life." (288). As Louise gazes from her window her focus is drawn to "patches of blue sky." This patch of blue sky is referenced as a symbol of positive feelings about her future without her husband that begin to invade her thoughts. Chopin writes, "There was something coming to her and she was waiting for it, fearfully. What was it? She did not know; it was too subtle and elusive to name. But she felt it, creeping out of the sky, . . ." (288). Evidence of Louise's feelings of joy become obvious when she says "free, free, free!" (288). The depiction of the clouds that surround Louise's "patch of blue" sky are critical in expressing the temporary passage of sorrow. "There were patches of blue sky showing here and there through the clouds that had met and piled one above the other in the west facing her window" (288). The gathering of the clouds in the west is synonymous with the sun rising in the east and setting in the west, and symbolizes the passage of her grief.

Furthermore, "The Story of an Hour" often reflects sorrow. Chopin begins her story with "Knowing that Mrs. Mallard was afflicted with a heart trouble, great care was taken to break to her as gently as possible the news of her husband's death." (287). The reader is initially expected to accept this "heart trouble" as a physical ailment. After having read the entire story, the reader should assume that the "heart trouble" is an example of double entendre and is indicative of her feelings toward her position in life as a married woman—as a possession rather than as an individual. The burden of "physical exhaustion" that "presses her down" into the armchair "haunted her body and seemed to reach into her soul" is a subtle use of symbolism (288). This reinforces the idea of the burden Louise feels from being seen only as a wife rather than an individual. During beginning of the climax of the story Louise leaves her room with ". . .a feverish triumph in her eyes, and she carried herself unwittingly like a goddess of Victory. She clasped her sister's waist, and together they descended the stairs" (289). This descent down the stairs is the final physical act that the protagonist Louise takes part in before her life meets a sudden end when she sees that her husband Brently is, in fact, still alive. This might be intended to be a parallel to the idea of the religious belief of passing down to her previous state of purgatory that she feels that she is trapped in prior to receiving the news of her husband's death.

Brently Mallard's description is evidence of additional symbolism that reflects Louise's feelings of sorrow. Chopin writes: "It was Brently Mallard who entered, a little travel-stained, . . ." (289). "Travel-stained" can be viewed by the reader as an example of symbolic double entendre. Louise may view her husband as "travel-stained" from possible past hardships in their marriage or simply weathered or stale from the passage of their time together. "He had been far from the scene of the accident, and did not even know there had been one" refers not only to the train accident that he reportedly perished in, but also to the accident of Louise's discovery that she might have more enjoyable future as a widow. The final implementation that brings about the end of the climax by utilizing irony is in the final paragraph. "When the doctors came they said that she had died of heart disease—of joy that kills." (289). Almost too typically, the male doctors assume that Louise dies from her heart disease or from a "troubled heart." It was in fact the shock of instantly losing her new-found sense of individuality that ended her life, along with losing the hope for a future to truly call her own.

The symbolism in "The Story of an Hour" is the essential element that allows for the character development for the protagonist Louise Mallard. "And yet she had loved him—sometimes. Often she had not. What did it matter! What could love, the unsolved mystery, count for in face of this possession of self-assertion which she suddenly recognized as the strongest impulse of her being!" (288). Chopin's use of symbolism illustrates Louise Mallard's internal struggle between her sorrow at the loss of her husband, and the bliss born from the realization that she desires a future where she would belong to only herself.

Work Cited

Chopin, Kate. "The Story on an Hour." *Literature: An
Introduction to Reading and Writing*. 4th Compact
Edition. Upper Saddle River, NJ: Pearson, 2008. 287-
289. Print.

Through Pain Love Can Be Found

Thu-Trang Pham
ENGL 1102
♦♦♦

Everywhere in the world, people naturally have their own dreams and desires that they really wish to achieve. However, it is not very easy to figure out what is important in life. Thus, while some people know from the start what they want to obtain, others have a difficult times trying to find out what their purpose is in life. Likewise, the narrator in Fight Club, by Chuck Palahniuk, at first has no idea what the meaning of his life is. Consequently, to escape the consumer culture which drowns him in the unreal, lonely, and meaningless of life, the narrator unconsciously creates and uses his split personality, Tyler Durden, to form Fight Club so that he can be able to feel alive and thus understand what is really important to him.

Living in the consumer culture, the narrator realizes that his lonely life is totally meaningless. Because he lives in a culture where consumerism dominates, there is only one thing that matters: money. More specifically, going to the car crashes and accidents to decide whether he should do a recall or not—the narrator earns money by placing peoples' lives in the equation of life and death: "If X is greater than the cost of a recall, we recall the cars and no one gets hurt. If X is less than the cost of a recall, then we don't recall" (Palahniuk 30). Indeed, Suzanne Del Gizzo agrees that the narrator's job is "dehumanization" (77). Truly, all people care about is the things and goods that they can buy and possess such as IKEA furniture, and the narrator is no exception. Actually, he acknowledges that he is the "slave to [his] nesting instinct" (Palahniuk 43). Indeed, Del Gizzo asserts that instead of being the controllers, the people, including the narrator, grow up a society where consumerism manipulates them (70).

Undoubtedly, living alone in the world where he only works and then blindly buys things, the narrator definitely lacks the most important thing in the world—relationships. As a result, he unconsciously tries to find what he does not have out of those senseless, motionless things that he buys. Indeed, it is absolutely true as Terry Lee approves that the narrator unknowingly uses the IKEA furniture as a substitute for "human relationships" (418), or according to Del Gizzo, the narrator only uses those things to replace the emptiness and "help him establish his sense of self" (76). Nevertheless, after spending his whole life to get all of that, he is still the same lonely person who has no feeling because he never experiences a real relationship; thus, he is still unable to feel alive.

Furthermore, the narrator is also lost in the unreal and meaningless world. To him, everything is meaningless because what he has done up until now is not what he really wants. Initially, the reason he goes to college is because"[his] father never [went] to college so it's really important [he goes] to college," or he has a job and get married because his father says so (Palahniuk 50-51). Thus, although he lives, he lives like a robot that automatically moves and does things indifferently and without feeling. In addition, the narrator is also trapped in an empty world where people live following the only pattern of life: going to college, getting a job, earning money, and finally sinking deeply into the consumer culture. Everyone, including himself, is identical, like "a copy of a copy of a copy" of each other (Palahniuk 21). Moreover, like the "no real food" in his fridge, nothing feels real to him, and his lonely life always goes with "tiny single-serving" things such as "single-serving butter" or "tiny single-serving friend" (Palahniuk 28, 31, 49). Therefore, only surrounded by all the lifeless non-living things, the narrator lives an isolated, solitary, and meaningless life with no relationship. As Del Gizzo affirms, "the 'single-serving' state of mind has come to dominate his life" (77). Consequently, the narrator is drawn into a blurry and unreal world where everything is indistinguishable. And as Del Gizzo again admits, "The narrator seems unable to experience his life as real at all" (89).

As a result, the loneliness and meaninglessness finally drive him to his insomnia, which is also the reason he goes to the support groups, the cause of the existence of his split personality, Tyler Durden, and the establishment of Fight Club.

Because of the insomnia, the narrator unconsciously creates and uses his split personality, Tyler Durden, to form Fight Club so that he can become real and feel life. At the beginning, when the insomnia just starts, the narrator only goes to the support groups, the places where people who have lethal illnesses and diseases gather to confide in each other, and uses them as a means to cure his insomnia. However, exactly as the narrator confirms, "I [feel] more alive than [I've] ever felt"; to feel alive is his real reason to join the groups (Palahniuk 22). According to Del Gizzo, only when he goes to the support groups "where he is touched," the narrator believes that he becomes "a part of something vital and significant" (77). Thus, he can finally feel like he's alive and able to escape his unreal and meaningless life.

However, the feeling soon is ruined when Marla Singer attends the support groups. As hugging helps him feel alive, crying is also the way the narrator gets in touch with himself and is able to sleep. Nevertheless, after Marla appears in the groups, the narrator admits that he "can't cry with [her] watching [him]" (Palahniuk 22); thus, he is unable to sleep like before. He now can longer go to the support groups because of Marla's presence. Consequently, the moment the insomnia comes back to him, he also steps back to where he tries to escape his unreal and meaningless world. Nonetheless, the feeling of wanting to become real and alive now grows even stronger, leading to the creation and existence of the Fight Club.

At last, the narrator can be able to feel alive again with the physical contact and the pain he goes through at the Fight Club. Obviously, there is only one thing people do at the Fight Club, which is fighting; apparently, the only sensation they can feel is the pain from the injuries. Thus, it is extremely contradictory when the narrator proclaims, "You aren't alive anywhere like you're alive at fight club" (Palahniuk 51). Therefore, it distinctly proves that the narrator, through the feeling of pain, can really feel alive and realize his own existence. Indeed, as Asbjorn Gronstad affirms: "Pain means to be 'directly exposed to being'." Furthermore, like how people pinch themselves to know whether they are asleep or awake, the narrator, by getting himself hurt, seemingly tries to use the pain as a way to wake himself up from the illusory world and thus to give him the real sense of living. Bülent Diken and Carsten Bagge Laustsen also agree: "Through physical pain a sublime body arises: a living body" (65). Besides the pain, the physical contact in Fight Club also brings the narrator to life as he fights. Similar to the hugging activity in the support groups, the physical contact, which is fighting with "no shoes no shirts" at Fight Club, helps him feel alive and get away from his unreal world (Palahniuk 50). Indeed, as Del Gizzo asserts, it's "physical intimacy designed to give a clear sense of self in a hypermediated, unreal society" (90).

As a result, transforming from a motionless, lifeless self who has no feeling and is always alone living in an empty world, the narrator, through Fight Club, now can become real and alive and thus be able to obtain the thing he lacks—relationships. Although the narrator always believes that it is Tyler who loves Marla, he unknowingly has feeling for Marla at the very beginning when he first meets her. Indeed, Del Gizzo confirms that because they "under false pretenses" have the same motive of joining the support groups, which is to feel alive, the narrator, "without noticing their similarities or his attraction to [Marla]," becomes worried and pestered with her presence (77). Furthermore, because he was unable to experience his own life before, there is no way he can realize the feeling he has for another person. Nonetheless, since he, through Fight Club, can escape from his blurry world, everything becomes real to him. Consequently, the feeling he has for Marla gradually appears clearer once he is able to feel alive. From the one who once wishes to "watch Marla die" because she gets Tyler's attention, the narrator unknowingly grows to care about Marla and wants "to warm her up, to make her laugh," and to save her life, realizing that he loves her (Palahniuk 60, 106).

Thus, his life is no longer meaningless because he now knows what is important to him. At the moment the narrator becomes conscious, realizing that Tyler is his split personality and discovering Tyler's intention with Project Mayhem, he desperately wants to stop Tyler by destroying him. In addition, the narrator is afraid that Tyler may kill Marla because she "[sees] Tyler Durden kill someone"; thus, he decides to kill

Tyler, even though that means he has to kill himself (Palahniuk 196). Therefore, by destroying Tyler, the narrator's decision appears very clearly as a choice to protect their relationship by sacrificing his life for the one he loves—Marla. Hence, at the moment he declares to Marla, "I'm trying to save your life!..because I think I like you," the narrator already makes his decision (Palahniuk 196-197). Renee D. Lockwood acknowledges that the narrator makes a "noble decision to shoot himself in the head in an attempt to rid the world of Tyler Durden's ferocity" (327). This act shows that the narrator now truly understands that protecting the one he loves is what is important in life. Therefore, escaping from his lonely and unreal world and thus being able to feel alive by the pain that he gets from Fight Club, the narrator's life is no longer meaningless because he has something important to protect and sacrifice for.

Through the pain he receives while fighting at Fight Club, the narrator in Fight Club can finally feel alive. His life is no longer meaningless because he now understands what is important to him. Hence, even if it means he must destroy himself, he still chooses to kill Tyler Durden—his split personality—to protect Marla, the one he loves. From a lonely person who has no feeling, who only knows how to work, and then is drowned in consumer culture, he now willingly sacrifices his life without regret, for he obtains what he always lacked before—relationships.

Works Cited

Del Gizzo, Suzanne. "The American Dream Unhinged: Romance
    and Reality in The Great Gatsby and Fight Club." *F.
    Scott Fitzgerald Review* 6.1 (2008): 69-94. Literary
    Reference Center. EBSCO. Web. 19 Oct. 2011.

Diken, Bülent, and Carsten Bagge Laustsen. "Enjoy Your Fight!
    – Fight Club as a Symptom of the Network Society."
    Genre, Gender, Race, and World Cinema. Ed. Julie F.
    Codell. Massachusetts: Blackwell Publishing, 2007. 56-
    7. Web. 22 Oct. 2011.

Gronstad, Asbjorn. "One-dimensional Men: Fight Club and the
    Poetics of the Body." *Film Criticism* 28.1 (2003): 1+.
    Literature Resource Center. Web. 20 Oct. 2011.

Lee, Terry. "Virtual Violence in Fight Club: This Is What
    Transformation of Masculine Ego Feels Like." *Journal
    of American & Comparative Cultures* 25.3/4 (2002):
    418-423. Academic Search Complete. EBSCO. Web. 22
    Oct. 2011.

Lockwood, Renee D. "Cults, Consumerism, and the Construction
    of Self: Exploring the Religious within Fight Club."
    Journal of Contemporary Religion 23.3 (2008): 321-335
    . Academic Search Complete. EBSCO. Web. 22 Oct.
    2011.

Palahniuk, Chuck. *Fight Club*. New York: W.W. Norton,
    1996. Print.

***

Why I Like This Essay: Thu-Trang wrote a number of
excellent essays for my ENGL1102 class. Of them all, this essay
stands out the most because of her original thinking. Her
research is well-done and thorough, and her ideas are expressed
clearly, not an easy feat for a novel that is difficult to interpret.
What makes this essay even more remarkable is that Thu-Trang's
first language is not English. The fact that she was able to write
this essay so well and so clearly is a testament to her persistence
and hard work.
Marissa McNamara, Assistant Professor of English

Enemy Land

Ana Smith
ENGL 1102H

If the United States had only fought the Viet Cong (VC) and North Vietnamese Army (NVA) in the Vietnam War, the United States probably would have won outright. While the United States had a world-renowned fighting force for much of the 20th Century, most of Vietnam did not even have indoor plumbing; yet the United States still failed to secure its goal of keeping South Vietnam out of Communist control. Although the U.S.'s defeat may seem bizarre from a distance, the American infantry soldier fighting in the jungles and rice paddies of Vietnam perceived the enemies that made the Vietnam War an impossible fight for America. Moreover, the infantrymen were pivotal to the American strategy in Vietnam, and how they perceived the enemy influenced how well the rest of the armed forces could fight. Many American infantry men viewed the Vietnamese land, the Vietnamese people, and American generals as enemies in addition to the most realized enemies, the VC and NVA.

The land was a prominent yet subtle enemy to the American infantry soldier. In Vietnam War literature, Vietnam veterans describe VC and NVA attacks as if the attacks originated in the land. Tim O'Brien employs this indicative language in The Things They Carried at two points in the story—when Lieutenant Cross recalls a nighttime firefight and when Mitchell Sanders describes being on a listening patrol. In Lieutenant Cross's recollection of the firefight, the language indicates that the land includes the elements that can kill soldiers. Lieutenant Cross recalls that "the field just exploded. Rain and slop and shrapnel, it all mixed together and the field seemed to boil" (162). Here, O'Brien mixes the elements of attack with the natural elements in such a way that he renders the human enemy invisible and the terrain a lethal attacker or weapon. Although O'Brien may not have been conscious of this metaphor, his writing does show signs that he, at least subconsciously, thought of the land as an enemy.

At another point in the book, this same style of language reappears when O'Brien relates Mitchell Sander's story of a listening patrol in the mountains. Sanders urgently struggles to make O'Brien "understand" that "everything talks. The whole country. Vietnam. The place talks" (71). The land's personification allows it to achieve a more tangible, human status, thereby endowing the land with intent. And what other intent could it have than to rid itself of foreign invaders with napalm, Agent Orange, and airplanes? Perhaps Sanders meant to say in his story that Vietnam—the land—had its own intentions, and it harbored a grudge against the American soldiers. The listening patrol soldiers in Sanders' story feel this so strongly that they call in a full-fledged attack on the jungle. In the words of Mitchell Sanders, "They make jungle juice" (71). By itself the prevalent use of defoliants such as Agent Orange during the Vietnam War suggests that the American military widely viewed the jungle as a threat to victory.

If an infantry soldier felt antagonism against the land, the antagonism often developed before the soldier engaged in combat or passed through the jungle on patrols. According to Christian Appy, a number of Vietnam veterans remember "a foul odor" and oppressive heat greeting them on their arrival, and this startling combination made the soldiers feel "defiled and unclean" from their first introduction to the country. The tropical heat of Vietnam contributed to the smell's intensity, but accounts of the smell's cause and nature vary according to soldiers. Appy indicates that some soldiers believed the U.S. cause the smell by burning waste, while other soldiers attributed the smell to the lack of plumbing in Vietnam. In the end, most soldiers agreed that some awful odor permeated Vietnam (127-128). Whatever the cause, a number of American soldiers were immediately pitted against the land upon their arrival. This negative impression combined with others' impressions of Vietnam left an overall unpleasant view of the country for the American infantry soldier. While the smell and heat did not solely elevate the land to enemy status, they did help the military paint the adversarial picture of the land. And a less attractive land is somewhat easier to destroy.

After their first hot, smelly encounter with Vietnam, many American infantry soldiers painfully and sometimes lethally acquired more substantial reason to hate the Vietnamese terrain. Combat and patrol accounts from infantrymen show the contention between American soldiers and the land. Michael Kelly, a machine gunner in the infantry, sums up the conditions of a patrolling infantry soldier: "You were always filthy, always soaking wet, freezing or roasting your butt off...leeches in the trees...bugs of every sort crawling all over you...jungle rot on your arms...sleeping on rocks; sleeping in the rain...never sleeping...slipping and sliding in the muck..." (qtd. in Endelman 194-195). Without guns or grenades or other human weapons, the land made small, sustained attacks. If not killing or injuring them through disease or animals, it gnawed at American soldiers' energy reserves. By gradually weakening the soldiers, the land strengthened the Viet Cong and North Vietnamese Army. As Appy suggests, a weary, hungry soldier distracted by the unfamiliar environment is more likely to step on a booby-trap or walk into an ambush than a well-rested, alert soldier familiar with the terrain and its hazards (170).

But one cannot blame the land completely for its ominous reputation. American soldiers hated the land in part because of the tactics of the North Vietnamese Army and especially those of the Viet Cong. Appy points out that the American strategy involved staying hidden in the jungle and ambushing American troops (146-147). Unable to see their enemy, American soldiers would often shoot into the jungle blindly, hoping to hit the person shooting at them. The American soldier must have thought that the animals were snipers or that the trees were cradling machine guns somewhere. Although the guerrillas or NVA regulars were likely behind the attack, many American infantry soldiers still felt that the land made its own offenses.

Appy also notes that the Viet Cong were particularly skilled in setting booby-traps (146-147). By leaving mines and booby-traps and by taking advantage of their knowledge of the land, the VC embedded itself into the land to such an extent that

American troops could not distinguish between human fighters and the land. Directly but more indirectly, the terrain was a lethal enemy to the American combat soldier, and the soldier was wise to remember this.

While the land significantly aided the VC and NVA assault on American forces, the South Vietnamese, willingly and unwillingly, also played the part of the enemy at times. Some South Vietnamese civilians' attitudes toward American troops convinced the troops that the soldiers were unwelcome occupiers instead of celebrated saviors, thereby initializing the contention. Peter S. Kindsvatter asserts that American soldiers realized that the South Vietnamese people resented the soldiers' presence. Kindvatter also suggests that American soldiers were not saviors in the minds of some Vietnamese, but rather armed money bags or unwelcome occupiers that should be killed (143-144). In front of the public, many of the top politicians and generals running the war claimed that American troops were dying in order help the South Vietnamese repulse the Communist North. But many American troops had to turn back and ask, "Who's the enemy?" Ironically, the South Vietnamese inspired some of the American soldiers' anger by not succumbing to the same death that many American soldiers did. According to Appy, American soldiers hated the Vietnamese in part because "civilians rarely stepped on land mines yet almost always claimed to lack any knowledge that mines had been set in and around their villages." This terribly frustrated the American soldiers because land mines were highly effective tools that the VC used to kill the troops (168-169). As if sensing loaded dice, many of the American soldiers who had any trust for civilians quickly lost it, and many of the already suspicious soldiers guarded themselves more carefully.

But on occasion, the Vietnamese civilians deserved the American soldiers' suspicions. Appy points out that villagers, sympathizing with the VC/NVA, helped the VC/NVA build and plant "land mines and booby- traps" (168-170). Although not officially a part of the VC/NVA fighting force, the civilians did participate in actions against the troops; thus the troops had a valid reason to view the citizens as enemies. However, Le Ly Hayslip argues that the VC often threatened civilians by sending "death squads" to kill those who the VC suspected killed American or South Vietnamese forces (142-143). Thus, a number of civilians who did help the VC may not have done so willingly or from conviction. However, widespread and degrading opinions of the Vietnamese people may have obscured this fact, and many American soldiers held to the belief that almost all Vietnamese people were enemies.

The fact that many VC fought in civilian clothing and used women and children as cover or as fighters only deepened the chasm of enmity between American soldiers and South Vietnamese villagers. In his poem "Guerilla War," Vietnam veteran W.D. Ehrhart explains the trouble distinguishing harmless civilians from Viet Cong soldiers: "They tape grenades/ inside their clothes/ and carry satchel charges/ in their market baskets./ Even their women fight and young boys / and girls." Twice in the poem he writes, "It's practically impossible/ to tell civilians/ from Viet Cong;/ after a while,/ you quit trying" (61). How could the soldiers fight the enemy and protect civilians if the enemy and civilians flowed into each other like water? Kindsvatter supports Ehrhart's assessment of fighting in Vietnam by writing that "sorting out innocent civilians from enemy combatants was even more pronounced [when compared to the World Wars and the Korean War] during the Vietnam War…Against an Asian foe who refused to fight fair, Americans tended to shoot first and take prisoners, or ascertain civilian status, later" (209). Some American soldiers rejected the frustrating and dangerous task of distinguishing harmless Vietnamese civilians from enemy fighters or sympathizers. In the eyes of many American soldiers, all Vietnamese people, innocent or not, became enemies.

The difficulty in distinguishing the VC/NVA from civilians and the military training combined to endow the American soldier with the grim view of the Vietnamese people. The American military trained soldiers to see the VC/NVA as sub-human pests worthy of death. According to Vietnam veteran Kurt Munson, "[Boot camp training] tended to dehumanize the enemy, to portray them as fodder, just somebody we needed to go and kill" (113). Because many troops found it difficult to separate the VC from civilians, this opinion overtook soldiers' opinion of civilians like black mold.

But American combat soldiers' enemies were not limited to Vietnamese origin. According to Appy, American soldiers often did not trust the top military personnel (184). It is not difficult to understand the soldiers' feelings on the matter when Appy further points out that part of the American military's strategy was to send ground troops on patrols to engage the enemy. Once they found the enemy, the soldiers called in the firepower of "jets and gunships and artillery" to obliterate the enemy, but many or all of the soldiers could die in the attack. Many soldiers, realizing and resenting their baiting role, developed a hatred for those military leaders who would risk the lives of their men to secure a promotion (182-184). Occasionally, troops would kill their own officers with fragmentation grenades in what are known as "fraggings." Endelman argues that fraggings were far less common than the media reported (209), but their existence leads one to suspect that other soldiers tacitly supported it. Former Marine Corps prosecutor Gary Solis, when considering the Vietnam War homicide rate, points out that in Vietnam, drugs, racial tension, and the draft put pressure on American troops that only served to increase anger towards those in authority (qtd. in Gregg and Alan).

With their goal to stay alive, many American soldiers felt they faced a horde of enemies in Vietnam. The land was a constant threat in its own right, pushing soldiers toward exhaustion and occasionally death. Other times it was a weapon the VC or NVA could use to ambush unwary American soldiers. The Vietnamese civilians received their enemy status through just and unjust assumptions of American soldiers and through the actions of VC/NVA sympathizers. Desperate to track down the elusive enemy, the American military high command turned into the American soldier's enemy by using them as bait to lure the enemy into fights. With their attention and aggression divided among so many enemies, the American soldier could not focus exclusively on the VC or NVA; and these enemies helped precipitate the American military's failure in Vietnam.

Works Cited

Appy, Christian G. Working Class War: American Combat
   Soldiers and Vietnam. Chapel Hill: University of
   North Carolina Press, 1993. Print.

Ehrhart, W.D. "Guerrilla War." From Both Sides Now: The
   Poetry of the Vietnam War and Its Aftermath.
   Ed. Philip Mahoney. New York: Scribner, 1998. Print.

Endelman, Bernard. "On the Ground: The U.S. Experience."
   Rolling Thunder in a Gently Land: The Vietnam War
   Revisited. Ed. Andrew Weist. Oxford: Osprey, 2006.
   Print.

Gregg, Zoroya and Alan Gomez. "War-zone Massacre and
   Uncommon Event." USA Today n.d.: Academic
   Search Complete. EBSCO. Web. Mar. 2011.

Hayslip, Le Ly and Dien Pham. "Caught in the Crossfire: The
   Civilian Experinece." Rolling Thunder in a Gentle Land:
   The Vietnam War Revisited." Ed. Andrew Weist.
   Oxford: Osprey, 2006. Print.

Kindsvatter, Peter S. American Soldiers: Ground Combat in the
   World Wars, Korea, and Vietnam. Lawrence, Kansas:
   University Press of Kansas, 2003. Print.

Munson, Kurt. "And Then They're Gone...Just Like That."
   Voices from the Vietnam War: Stories from
   American, Asian, and Russian Veterans. Xiaobing Li.
   Lexington, Kentucky: University Press of
   Kentucky, 2012. Print.

O'Brien, Tim. The Things They Carried. Boston:
   Mariner=Houghton Mifflin Harcourt, 1990. Print.

***

Why I Like This Essay: Ana Smith was in my Honors English
II course where she distinguished herself as an excellent writer
and student. This paper is a representation of her writing and
critical thinking abilities. What I am most impressed with is that
originality of her main point. Additionally, the paper is original,
well-researched, and well-written. Such a creative topic is not
easy to prove clearly, and Ms. Smith has clearly achieved this.
Marissa McNamara, Assistant Professor of English

On Simpler Things

Madison Kiley
ENGL 2111
◆◆◆

According to Wendy Swartz in her article "Rewriting a Recluse," I am "widely considered one of China's greatest poets"—and though I am humbled by this, I am also rather shocked (77). When I look around today, I see so many moving pictures—movies—that display, with my every inhalation, another great explosion. I see massive metal cages moving swiftly, darting like fish among each other on coal black paths. I see so many things that are strange to me—everything moving quickly, people rushing, and so much stress that I am left questioning why. Why am I, Tao Qian, with my simple poems, among the greatest writers of the past? Above all, however, I have to question this: what has happened to the value of simplicity? In this world, is simplicity considered something dull or unimportant? With this question in mind, I will be discussing three reasons why simplicity may be more vital to human life than any of this haste and constant action. These reasons concern nature, balancing the self, and finding Utopia.

One reason why it is important to live a simple life is because it brings mankind closer to the natural world. Nature is a force which nurtures man, so it is imperative that we spend as much time possible with it and learn to show great respect for it. I, myself, had many struggles in trying to find my own time and place to appreciate this world. As Huo Jianying said in his article "Balancing Man and Nature in Traditional China," I "found [my]self constantly at odds with the bureaucracy" (60). Though I was born into a prominent family and was well-qualified for mant official jobs, I never held interest in living a life toiling away indoors and in uncomfortable clothing. I would much rather be fishing alone in a small boat, waiting patiently for the fish who would tug on the string I would use to pull him out. I would listen to the slow creaking of the old wooden boat and the "clap" of the waves as they struck its sides. This is the sort of life

I most wanted to live—at least for as many moments as possible because, as the critic Huo Jianying says, "man is just one of the myriad elements comprising nature, and all elements in nature are equal and should coexist peacefully and harmoniously" (60). Though you may claim to me that a life among the trees and fields and rivers is nothing short of boring, I assure you that there is some hard work involved. As Huo Jianying also stated, after I left the office, I came to "enjoy. . .the pastoral beauty of [my] surroundings and the unsophisticated, though sometimes demanding, country life" (61). Though it may have been difficult at times, when tending to fields in dirty clothes, or fishing in the river during a sudden thunderstorm, nature never ceased to provide me with inspiration for my poems.

Though I am well-known for nature poetry, I am well-aware that I am not the only poet who has tried—especially in my country—to translate the world's beauty into words. I have noticed that many of my fellow Chinese writers have practiced a skill that is, however, very unlike my own. Yim-Tze Kwong states that "at times even Li Bai's exalted valour seems a little dramatized and Du Fu's superb skill a shade artificial" but that my "poetry is almost unfailingly convincing in its direct lyricism and simple language" (36). I am quite humbled by that compliment, especially after I have had the chance to read some works by those great writers. It takes no true scholar to see that Du Fu's poem "Thousand League Poo," for example, has much in the way of eloquence with lines such as: "Oh, when shall the blazing skies of summer pass, / That his will may exult in the meeting of wind and rain" (1387). I compare this with one of my own works, "In the Sixth Month of 408, Fire," in which the last two lines are: "Since I was not born in such a time, / let me just go on watering my garden" (1367). Though I agree that Du Fu's poetry sounds all the more beautiful here, I cannot say that I think it more effective than my own. Of course there is artistic merit in the sweeping, emotional diction that Du Fu uses, but there is still one question in my mind. Is nature best described the way a mockingbird would sing it? Or the way a river and the wind and the willow trees would have it said? Though I do not believe that I am the authority on poetry, nor do I know much more about the natural world than the most inexperienced naturalist, I can say that I have to agree with the latter proposal. Even if one chooses the other route—that nature should be described as eloquently as possible—how does one describe the nature of the mockingbird—its erratic flight patterns and territorial habits—with any true elegance?

That is not to say that it is totally impossible for one to write about nature in a way that is interesting and beautiful, but simply that it is unnecessary. I believe that any word a human being could ever say or write as a description for nature would be likened to wrapping tree branches with paper. No man could ever improve on nature, so it is pointless to try and embellish any description of it, except in an effort to call forth appreciation and respect for the natural world. In other words, with all the technological advancements and the more contemporary works which try, with flowery yet superfluous phases to capture nature's essence, I would never give up describing it simply. Because the natural world never offers us complete sentences, why not do the trees and fields justice and leave spaces in your works and life for the wind to just blow through and the frogs' croaks to chime in? In the case of living a life close to nature, sometimes simplicity is the key.

Beyond the scope of nature, it is also important to live simply in order to balance the self. In this sense, it can be said that a person needs time to reflect—whether nature is involved or not. I have seen, for example, many critics who have labeled me as a "recluse" and describe my poems as having an "abiding sense of loneliness" (Kwong 36). When one is of a reclusive nature, it does not always mean that he is lonely and I did not intend to portray a sense of utter isolation in my poems. In this contemporary world, however, I see many people who live so much in social activities that they lose themselves in excess— excessive drinking, obscene behavior, and the like. I am not trying to discourage anyone from having a social life, nor am I trying to encourage one to be a recluse—I am merely describing the importance of a balance between the two. The majority of my poems, in fact, follow this balanced approach through a Daoist perspective. As Mary Bockover says of Daoism in the article "Daoism, Ethics & Faith," "good living is tied to attaining a spiritual perspective that lets one be at ease with, and in awe of, the natural course of events, even in the inevitable events of aging, illness, and death" (144). It is clear, then, that simplicity does not necessarily equate to dullness, but to complete acceptance and openness. On one hand, one must not struggle to escape others, and on the other hand, he must not strive too strongly to be constantly surrounded by them. Thus, the body becomes like a river, which flows without struggle between its shores and rises and falls as the seasons come and go. When the river becomes overly proud, it comes to overflow and sullies itself with drunkenness and debris. When the river comes to cynicism, it shrinks in loneliness until its last few drops are hidden beneath the dirt. So, my poems are not meant to be seen as examples of lonely misery, but instead to teach the importance of simplicity—in balance. The body is to be treated as the river, to ebb and flow naturally without excess or deficiency, for this is the Dao—The Way.

The final—and possibly most important—aspect of living simply is the art of finding one's own utopia. Take note here that a utopia is dissimilar from a paradise in that a paradise "is primarily a religious or mythical vision of happiness" (Chiang 97). A utopia, on the other hand, is described by Chiang as something where "human agency, rather than divine providence, is the driving force of social progress" (97). In other words, she claims that utopia is definitely something achievable by human efforts. One does not, however, tend to find such a place where life is full of chaos—which I see is often the case in most lives nowadays. That is where simplicity comes back into the picture. My work "Peach Blossom Spring," for example, explores this very idea of how simple living can bring one to find true happiness or one's own utopia. It is about a fisherman who happens upon a hidden community, cut off from the world and very prosperous because the inhabitants are self-sufficient and take great care of their beautiful land. Though the fisherman took great pains to record directions back to the location, no one else was ever successful in finding it. What this means is that utopia cannot be found through struggle or constant action, but with an open mind and a drifting spirit and consciousness into the unknown. This is the way I find utopia—in my poetry and writing. I do not know what beauty will unfold from my quiet reflection or the completion of a poem. Simple living, therefore, does not have to be dull living because, ultimately, it can lead a person into great and unexpected happiness.

When everything is said and done, what is most important is that a human being leads a successful and fulfilling life. What worries me about the lifestyle I see now is that so many people are in need of constant stimulation. What, now, is fulfilling to humanity but an excess of things? So many people feast excessively, buy things of greater material worth than practical use, destroy more land than they use, and seek out dangerous acts merely to shock others. Human beings strive so strongly to escape the ordinary, the dull, and the simple—when these may be the very things that would bring them the most happiness. Sometimes one needs to merely sit beside a river and listen to the water running over rocks, or to confess to oneself one's deepest secrets in a poem. With all this excess and chaos leading so many to stress and sickness, it may be time to find value in simple things, such as spending time in nature, finding a balance, and creating your own version of utopia in everything you do.

Works Cited

Bockover, Mary I. "Daoism, Ethics & Faith." *Journal of Daoist Studies* 4 (2011): 139-153. Academic Search Complete. Web. 9 April 2011.

Chiang, Sing-Chen Lydia. "Visions of Happiness: Daoist Utopias and Grotto Paradises in Early and Medieval Chinese Tales." *Utopian Studies* 20.1 (2009): 97-120. Academic Search Complete. Web. 10 March 2011.

Ch'ien, T'ao. "In the Sixth Month of 408." *The Norton Anthology of World Literature*. 2nd ed. Vol. B. New York: W. W. Norton, 2002. 1367. Print.

Fu, Du (Tu). "Thousand League Pool." *The Norton Anthology of World Literature*. 2nd ed. Vol. B. New York: W. W. Norton, 2002. 1387. Print.

Jianying, Huo. "Balancing Man and Nature in Traditional Culture." *China Today* 57.5 (2008): 60-63. Academic Search Complete. Web. 15 March 2011.

Kwong, Yim-Tze. "Naturalness and Authenticity: The Poetry of Tao Qian." *Chinese Literature: Essays Articles, Reviews* 11 (1989):35-77. JSTOR. Web. 10 March 2011.

Swartz, Wendy. "Re-writing a Recluse: The Early Biographers' Construction of Tao Yuanming." *Chinese Literature: Essays, Articles, Reviews* 26 (2004): 77-97. JSTOR Web. 13 March 2011.

Social Injustices of William Blake's Era

Samuel Slappey
ENGL 2122
♦♦♦

William Blake was an English Romantic poet who lived from 1757 to 1827. There are many things that define Blake as a poet, such as his ability to draw and the fact that he illustrated all of his poems. One other important characteristic that distinguished Blake from many of his peers was his ability to address the social issues of his time. Blake railed against everything from the destruction of the natural beauty of England, to the treatment of children and laborers in the new English economy, to racism. Blake's poems in his collection *Songs of Innocence and of Experience* (1794) portray a social consciousness and initiative in the poet, and he is able to clearly demonstrate his points without dragging his poetry down into the mire of political stagnation. Blake's poetry is political without ruining the creative, artistic aspect of his craft, which is something that many artists throughout various formats fail to do. Important examples of Blake's politically charged poetry from these collections include "The Echoing Green," "The Chimney Sweeper," and "The Little Black Boy."

"The Echoing Green" is a poem which celebrates the beauty and significance of nature. It describes a green field where "The sky-lark and thrush/ The birds of the bush/ Sing louder around/ To the bells' chearful sound" (lines 5-8), and children run and play. Blake, like most of his contemporary Romantic poets, paints nature as a beautiful, idyllic contrast to the evil, corrupted cities. Perhaps "evil" isn't the right word, but it certainly isn't far away from the Romantic poet's view of industrialized society. "The Echoing Green" is Blake's tribute to the natural world and the way people who live simpler lives are able to interact with and appreciate nature without taking too much away from it. The poem also shows a sense of community in this green place where both the old and the young would gather together. This statement of the wonder of nature, apparent in "The Echoing Green," is also an indirect diatribe against the industrialization movement that was going on at the time, causing great harm to the surrounding natural environment and making Blake's picture of a perfect community a thing of the past. In a way, Blake is almost portraying the tragic aspect of industrialization, whether purposefully or by accident, in a more effective way than if he had directly talked about the harms and pollution an industrialized world brings. Instead, he glorifies the natural world and forces the reader to picture everything he or she would be losing if industrialization were to truly ruin that natural beauty.

There are actually two poems written by William Blake entitled "The Chimney Sweeper," in Songs of Innocence and of Experience. During William Blake's life, working conditions were very bad in most English cities. Workers were forced to work extremely long hours in harsh factory conditions with highly dangerous machinery and for very low wages, in large part because of the lack of labor laws that existed in England in the 1700's and early 1800's. Even worse, children were often forced to work in these conditions and subjected to work environments that could seriously harm them and damage their future health. Both of Blake's "The Chimney Sweeper" poems are social commentaries on the horrors of a job that children were routinely forced to work. Chimney sweepers were forced to climb up soot-filled chimneys and clean out the entire dirty residue of ash and soot stuck in them. The job was forced on children for several reasons. They were small enough to fit into the chimneys and be able to maneuver enough to clean, no adults wanted to clean chimneys for a living, and many of the chimney sweepers were literally sold into these lives of labor, so they didn't have much of a choice what work they would be doing. Boys as young as four years old were forced into this line of work where they could suffer numerous health risks. These risks included getting stuck in the extremely narrow chimney shafts where they could either suffocate or be burned, stunted growth and deformities, and loss of eyesight. In addition to these immediate health concerns, the soot in chimneys is a carcinogen, which means that it can cause cancer. Many chimney sweeps, if they survived their childhood, would go on to die later in life of lung cancer, or the black lung as it was referred to during the time of William Blake. Blake saw the horrendous life these boys were forced into and the two pieces he wrote on chimney sweepers decried the society that could let this happen to its youth. In the first chimney sweeper poem in *Songs of Innocence and of Experience*, lines like "When my mother died I was very young, /And my father sold me while yet my tongue/ Could scarcely cry ''weep! 'weep! 'weep! 'weep!'" (1-3) portray a loneliness and sense of abandonment that must have been felt by these child laborers. Still, while he mentioned the conditions and the hardships the chimney sweepers endured, Blake really focused on the fact that they wanted to get away from that life. Little Tom Dacre, the chimney sweep in the poem, dreams of an angel who frees "thousands of sweepers" (11), who run "down a green plain, leaping, laughing.../And wash in a river and shine in the sun" (15-16). This dream about a better place full of light and happiness where they will be loved is similar to the images represented by "The Echoing Green." The contrast that they see between this place and their real lives on earth is the truest indication that Blake can provide of how miserable they are in the lives they are forced to live and with the jobs they are forced to work.

Although slavery was abolished in England in 1772, seventeen years before Blake's *Songs of Innocence* (1789) was published, it wasn't abolished throughout the British Empire until 1833. And, despite the fact that slavery no longer existed in England, black people were not treated the same as whites. While Blake's "The Little Black Boy" doesn't discuss the hardships of being black in England in the eighteenth century, it does show the emotions of a black child that experiences those hardships. Throughout the poem, the narrator uses images of light and darkness to reflect racial differences: "White as an angel is the English child,/ But I am black as if bereav'd of light" (3-4). Everything the narrator says is an attempt to show that he is no different from his white countrymen, which in itself is not a terrible thing. The tragedy of the poem is the way in which he says it. He cries, "But O! my soul is white" (2) and tries to prove that he is English and white through and through, even though his mother was from the "southern wild"(1). The black boy in the poem seems to be ashamed of the color of his skin. He thinks that being black is synonymous with bad and so he must try desperately to show that he is no different from the others, that he is, in fact, white on the inside. Blake believes that he should not have to show it, and that the black boy really is the same as everyone else on the inside.

Blake's sense of political awareness and the messages he puts in his poems are vital to his persona as a poet, but what is more important is the way he is able to incorporate his social views into his writing. Blake hardly ever says anything directly; he avoids saying, for example, "Industrialization is bad. We need to stop it." Many artists and writers get bogged down in their social message when they try to spread it, but Blake manages to avoid this heavy-handedness in his writing. Instead, he shows the readers everything they have now, everything they could lose, and the readers sympathize with the subject. Whether it is the natural beauty in "The Echoing Green" or the little boys doomed to a short, hard life in "The Chimney Sweeper," it is hard not to become attached to the subject of Blake's poems, and once attached the reader will want to shield the real-world equivalent of these poems from the horrors Blake explores. Perhaps he or she, once inspired by the writing, will try to preserve the natural beauty of the landscape, or protect the little chimney sweeps that the poet describes so brilliantly. Blake's mission seems to be to create a love in his audience of nature, of the black boy trying desperately to fit in, and of the children working in those chimneys, so that the reader will work to prevent them from coming to harm. If, in fact, this was his true purpose, he succeeded. Many have been touched by his poetry, and society today has changed its view on the issues that he wrote about. Blake is one of the great poets of English Romanticism, and he should be recognized not only by his great poetic reputation, but also by his legacy of social contribution.

Works Cited

Blake, William. "The Chimney Sweeper". *The Norton Anthology of EnglishLiterature*. Ed. Stephen Greenblatt et al. 8th ed. Vol. 2. New York: Norton, 2006. 85. Print.

"The Echoing Green". *The Norton Anthology of English Literature*. Ed. Stephen Greenblatt et al. 8th ed. Vol. 2. New York: Norton, 2006. 82-83. Print.

"The Little Black Boy". *The Norton Anthology of English Literature*. Ed. Stephen Greenblatt et al. 8th ed. Vol. 2. New York: Norton, 2006. 84. Print.

***

Why I Like This Essay: The author of this essay, Sam Slappey, not only recognizes the artistry of William Blake's poetry, but also the power of art to effect social change. Sam explicates the poems in relation to the historical context in which they were written, thus enabling the reader to understand the significance of these seemingly simple poems. His essay demonstrates all the elements of effective writing, such as clarity, coherence, and development. I also appreciated his excellent vocabulary. In short, this paper is the product of a student who is both a sensitive, perceptive reader and a skillful writer.

Lynn Summer, Assistant Professor of English

Contributors

Richard Abdulai

Samuel Adeseye

Drew Bannister
Masters Christian Academy
Atlanta, Georgia

Adrian Caldwell
Brookwood High School
Snellville, Georgia

Joseph Coates
S. Gwinnett High School
Snellville, Georgia

Eduardo Jaen Diez

Joshua Emeter
Nigerian Turkish
International College
Abuja, Nigeria

Olivia Hightower
Atlanta, Georgia

Desiree' Hines
Newton High School
Covington, Georgia

Ashleigh Jones
Murray-Wright
High School
Detroit, Michigan

Madison Kiley
N. Gwinnett High School
Suwanee, Georgia

Jeong Kim
Forest Hills Northern
High School
Grand Rapids, Michigan

Samuel Lack
Riverwood High School
Sandy Springs, Georgia

Tan-Phu Le
J. Frank Dobie HS
Houston, Texas

Cassandra Lewis
Ensley High School
Birmingham, Alabama

Courtney Linden

Vincent McQueen
Emanuel County Institute
Twin City, Georgia

Stephanie Moore
Atlanta, Georgia

John Pearson
Paducah Tilghman
Paducah, Kentucky

Thu-Trang Pham
Duluth High School
Duluth, Georgia
Vincent Roberts
Maconaquah High School
Bunkee Hill, Indiana

Samuel Slappey
Milton High School
Milton, Georgia

Ana Smith

Adam Stern
Roswell High School
Roswell, Georgia

Katsiaryna Tamashevich
CCA
Chattanooga, Tennessee

Chachee Valentine
West Windsor-Plainsboro
High School South
West Windsor Township
New Jersey

Tiara Marie VanLowe
Warren Woods Tower
High School
Warren, Michigan

Aleksandr Wobeck
Riverwood High School
Atlanta, Georgia